The Cloudberry Coaching Method

The Cloudberry Coaching Method

Design, Build, and Launch Your Next Big Chapter

Brad Lekang

Advantage | Books

Published by Advantage Books, Charleston, South Carolina.
An imprint of Advantage Media.

Printed in the United States of America.

10 9 8 7 6 5 4 3 2 1

ISBN: 979-8-89188-185-3 (Paperback)
ISBN: 979-8-89188-186-0 (eBook)

Library of Congress Control Number: 2026900881.

Cover design by Matthew Morse.
Layout design by Ruthie Wood.

02-23-2026 4:22

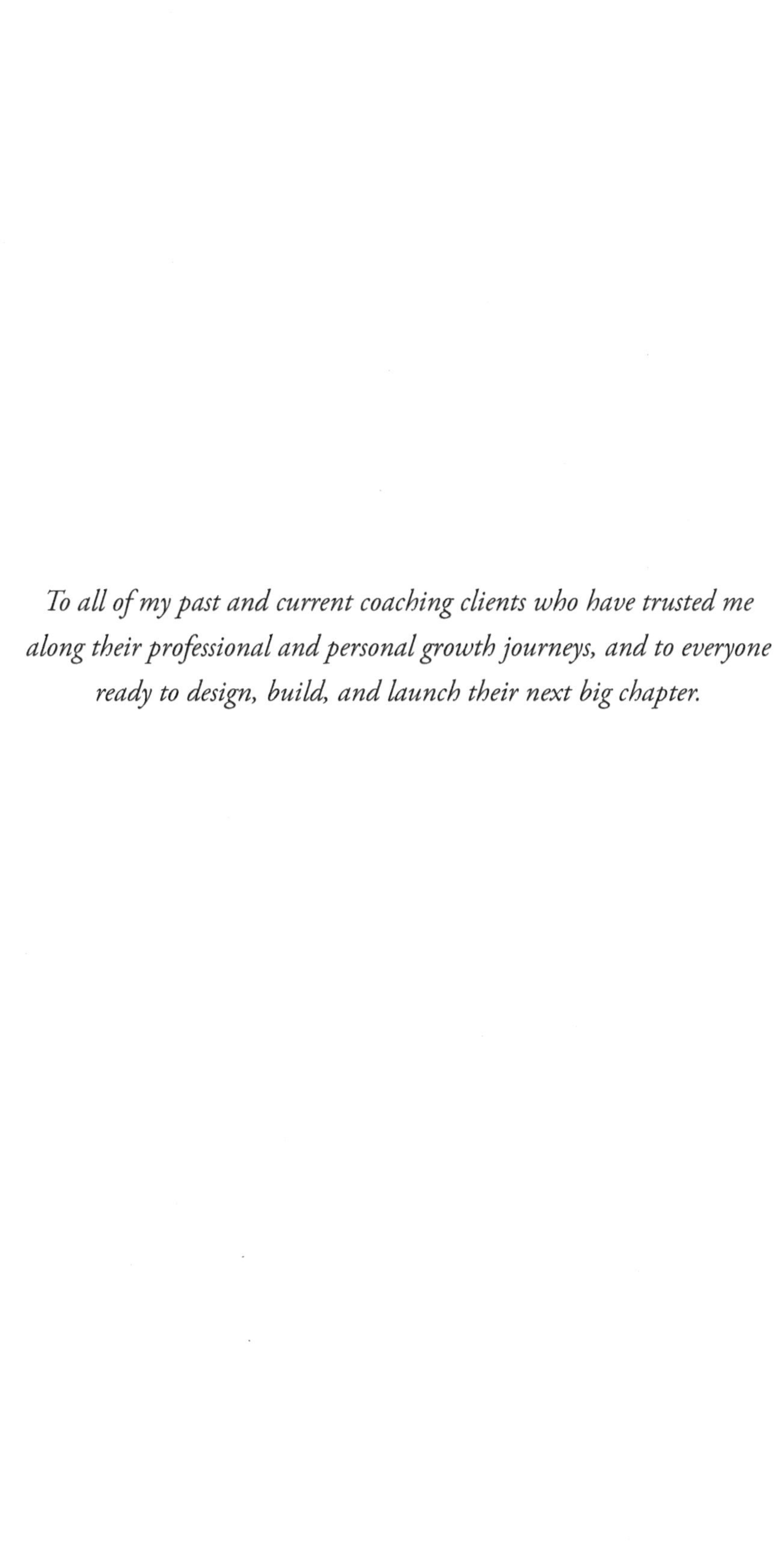

To all of my past and current coaching clients who have trusted me along their professional and personal growth journeys, and to everyone ready to design, build, and launch their next big chapter.

CONTENTS

ACKNOWLEDGMENTS

For inspiration, ideas, and encouragement to shoot for the stars, thank you to my masterful executive, leadership, and advanced neuroscience coaching gurus. Thank you for showing me the transformational power of coaching—an accelerant for growth and leadership—and the importance of building our next big chapters. Those years of coaching conversations didn't just help me succeed and push for the next summit; they shaped the way I coach, lead, and live. And to the mentors, allies, and champions who believed in me long before I fully believed in myself: Your support changed the trajectory of my career and my life. Your belief made all the difference.

For community and connection, thank you to my peer coaches whom I'm privileged to support in return, and to the guides and healers throughout my journey—far too many to name. Every single one of you has shaped who I am today and continues to influence the leader I am becoming.

For support, thank you to my family and friends who listened, challenged, celebrated, offered creative guidance, and kept me grounded through every pivot, setback, and leap forward. You know who you are.

For love and belief, thank you to my parents, Richard and Joyce, for modeling work ethic, integrity, humility, and care. You taught me that hard work and education are the path forward, that if you want something in life you better put in the hours and earn it, and that service to others—especially those less fortunate—is always part of the journey.

For love, patience, and being my daily sounding board, thank you to Ken. Thank you for twenty-six years and counting of unwavering support, especially on the day I came home with a few too many whiteboard sketches in hand and another big idea, announcing my dream to design, build, and launch a solopreneur adventure, when your reply was: "Let's go!" Through action and kindness, no one has taught me more about what it means to show up fully for someone, in sickness and in health.

And lastly, thank you to Hazel and Otis, our ten-year-old yellow Labrador littermates—my best hiking sidekicks, the most popular on-the-spot cuddle buddies to my officemates, and a constant source of joy and ridiculous entertainment for all.

INTRODUCTION

MY NEXT BIG CHAPTER

It's been said that the view from the summit is sweetest because of the climb. You climb the ladder, master the skills, and achieve what you wanted—only to discover that what got you here won't get you to the next big summit.

For me, that realization was the spark to design, build, and launch something new—a life built around alignment, freedom, and purpose, a framework that could hold my evolving priorities, my family's needs, and my professional ambitions.

That awareness brought me back to my roots. Growing up in Minneapolis, Minnesota, with parents shaped by North Dakota farm life, I was instilled with an unshakeable belief in the value of work, education, and resilience—not just as a measure of productivity but as a marker of character. And somewhere along the way, those very strengths—that adaptability—became the bridge I created to design, build, and launch my next big chapter.

Those lessons in character and resilience started early for me, long before I ever thought about leadership or a career. You see, when I was a boy and wanted a skateboard, some computer games, or money to go to the store, my parents were not ones to reach for their wallet or purse with a handout of easy money. Instead, I learned very early on that the only way to get what I wanted was to put myself to work, shoveling driveways in the snowy Midwestern winters and mowing lawns in the long, hot summers.

But it wasn't just the money I earned or even the things I bought that were the real reward of those grueling days. More importantly, I learned that working hard and being industrious were the way forward to get what I wanted and needed, to grow, and to earn my parents' admiration. My parents were always wonderful to me, but seeing the respect in their eyes as I trudged home with that first skateboard I saved for or frozen solid from a day of shoveling or covered in grass clippings after mowing—that meant the world to me.

And that connection between hard work and my sense of purpose and identity didn't stop at our front door. Throughout my childhood, those were values that our mostly Scandinavian-Norwegian neighborhood embraced and promoted.

For much of that time, five years to be exact, I awoke Monday through Friday at five in the morning before school to deliver newspapers for the *Minneapolis Tribune*, and I took great satisfaction in being the final link in the chain that was responsible for bringing everything that all of those reporters, editors, and photographers had put into the daily edition directly to my neighbors' front doorstep.

I remember one particular neighbor who bargained with me: If I delivered his newspaper before six every morning, when I went about collecting the accounts at the end of the week, he'd give me a big fat tip. If I missed a single morning deadline in a week, however—no matter the reason—there'd be no tip at all.

At the time, I thought he was just a very particular grown-up; maybe I even suspected that he was teasing me in some way I couldn't completely understand. Through the lens of hindsight, however, I can now clearly see that he was offering me a weekly lesson in the way of the world and the importance of taking care of business and being responsible. I understand his motivation and appreciate his efforts. And he always got his paper on time.

I learned a lesson that would later shape the Cloudberry Coaching Method (CCM) itself: Our choices and actions create our lives.

In the same way, I learned many valuable lessons in the rural town where my mother grew up—visiting the family farm, I learned early on where food really comes from. Eggs don't appear in a carton. Milk isn't sourced from a plastic jug. Chicken McNuggets don't originate in a freezer. Bacon doesn't start as strips in a package. I learned where food comes from because during all those trips from the city to the farms, I gathered it, helped raise it, and sometimes watched it be prepared firsthand.

I remember being no more than a child and standing beside my Grandpa Fred in a warm barn before sunrise, nervous to reach under a hen and gather the morning's eggs. He encouraged me—pushed me just enough—and I overcame that fear. That routine, and so many like it, became part of my childhood as we visited my grandparents: milking cows, gathering eggs and vegetables from the garden, shearing sheep, and watching my grandmother calmly and efficiently select and prepare the chicken that would be served at dinner that night. It was life on the farm—not just farm-to-table but barn-to-table.

These lessons I learned on the farm also began a deep respect for nature, ecosystems, and the relationship between humans and the environment. That awareness would later evolve into a personal passion for conservation, sustainability, responsibility, and balance—not just in nature but also in life and leadership.

As I said, I've been working since I was twelve, part-time or full-time, without a break. Whether it was delivering newspapers, mowing lawns, or washing dishes, I learned the value of effort and independence. My parents, both working-class professionals—my father an engineer, my mother an office administrator—matched my college savings dollar for dollar. If I saved, they matched. If I didn't, they didn't. That simple system taught me accountability, and I graduated from the University of Minnesota without a single student loan.

I worked various jobs: delivering newspapers, warehouse labor, stocking shelves, bagging groceries, and driving shuttle vans between hospitals. One formative period was my time at Kurt Manufacturing, in the summers during college, where I spent five grueling days a week handling thirty-pound metal computer cases in massive tumblers. It was hard, repetitive, physical work, but it taught me something I've never forgotten: Properly applied friction can lead to a perfect product. And the money I saved during the summer was matched by my parents for school the following year.

At the University of Minnesota, I spent four years as a competitive crew rower (think long skinny boats where each rower has one oar)—part of a team demanding physical and mental endurance. I wasn't the fastest. I wasn't the strongest. But I practiced thousands of hours on the water over four years and was often the last one to break. And this is how I made the first boat in my junior and senior years. I discovered I had a deep reservoir for grit, focus, and high-pressure performance. I wanted to win. I wanted to see what I was made of. Future visualization, a technique used by our coaches before every race, became a foundational part of my mindset. It's a practice I still use today in my coaching methodology.

After undergrad, I began my MBA in finance at the University of Minnesota and eventually earned a full-ride fellowship to attend Esade in Barcelona. My grades were high but not the best, and with only basic Spanish (and no Catalan) at the time, I was selected from the lengthy field of applicants not for academic perfection but for what the admissions team called "grit and determination—outworking everyone else." I embraced the challenges: language, culture, anticipated struggles. And I used them as fuel.

That's been a defining pattern throughout my life. I've taken on difficult work and steep challenges to push myself. To evolve. To test my mettle. To understand what's possible when effort meets intention.

And that's exactly what the CCM is built upon: the belief that transformation comes not only from moments of inspiration but also from a system built on clarity, courage, and the willingness to do the work.

When I graduated from grad school and stepped out into the real world, the professional landscape offered me an endless plane of opportunity and the chance to prove myself on a scale I'd never fully anticipated. The future seemed impossibly bright.

I started as a financial analyst with a local bank in Minneapolis, then took my freshly minted MBA and relocated to Denver to take a position with Visa. My time with Visa set me on a definitive path within the tech world, one focused on the specialty of online payment systems. I took those unique skills with me when I left for a position at Target Corporation—which involved a return home to Minneapolis, where I expected to stay for the long run. Like many best-laid plans, that idea shifted when I accepted the offer to work for Apple Inc. and moved to San Francisco, where I spent the next dozen years in Silicon Valley—a chapter of my life that would fundamentally shape everything that came next.

The average lifespan for each of us is just about seventy-eight years. And there are around two hundred billion others who have come before us, long since returned to the soil. And while that's what makes up our time here on Earth, it's funny how we can define our lives by just a handful of moments.

As the song goes, "Should I stay, or should I go?"

I had been exploring what my next big chapter might look like—toggling between ambition and uncertainty, working with coaches and mentors to think it through. Something deeper was whispering: What's next? This summit: It's not my final peak.

Still without a clear answer, I booked a solo trip to New Mexico—to the edge of the Navajo Nation and into the surreal silence of the Bisti/De-Na-Zin Wilderness.

On the first day, our Navajo guide asked where we were from. When I said San Francisco, he smiled knowingly.

"Another techie, I presume?"

"Yes, indeed," I replied.

"We get a lot of you out here, seeking to completely unplug. These badlands, they're about as far from Silicon Valley as you can get—the hoodoos, the wind-carved labyrinths, the awe-inspiring natural wonders that exist nowhere else."

It felt like he wasn't just seeing where I was from. He was seeing why I was there—even before I could say it myself.

Together, we wandered into the heart of the badlands. There are no marked trails—just wind-carved stone, sunbaked sandstone structures, forty-million-year-old petrified logs, and an unrelenting quiet. And then, in the middle of that vast stillness, I saw it: a beautiful old Piñon pine tree, improbably rooted in the rock.

I stopped.

It was twisted and thriving. It was alive, and it was anchored. It had found a way to grow in the harshest of places—not by resisting but by adapting. By bending to the elements rather than fighting them. Still. Grounded. Resilient.

I stared at that tree, and I swear—it stared back.

And in that moment, something surfaced from deep inside me. Growing up in Minnesota, I learned that where there's pine, there's water. The pine finds it—not on the surface but hidden beneath, where roots dig deep and steady. When you're lost in the wild, that's the rule: Look for the pine. There's water. There's life.

That tree had done just that. In the harshest terrain, it had found a way to thrive by staying rooted to what was beneath the surface but essential.

For a long time, I stood there. The tree. The hoodoos. The silence. The wind. The whole alien beauty of the Bisti Badlands. And something shifted.

It was a breakthrough. Absolute clarity.

That tree, that guide, that wilderness—they showed me something I hadn't seen in a while: The next summit doesn't come to you. You must design it. You must actively create your next big chapter.

And I knew exactly what I had to do.

CHAPTER ONE

THE TRANSITION

From a thirty-thousand-foot perspective, the professional migration I've undertaken makes perfect sense. My next move was not only aligned with my life's work but was also a natural extension of the elements to which I've devoted my career.

It was a journey from corporate tech and engineering to alignment—alignment with a shifting purpose and mission.

In many conversations, there's often a moment—sometimes silent, sometimes not—when I can see a question being formed and taking shape in someone's mind: How does this career shift make sense for you? How does someone who spent decades on the technical side of the corporate world, leading teams and solving complex global challenges, suddenly take a hard left turn into executive leadership coaching?

It's a fair question.

On the surface, the connection may not be obvious. One career is defined by leadership and bringing the solutions, systems, and execution. The other revolves around conversation, connection, identity, and the intangible language of growth. But what I've come to understand is that transformation isn't always about stepping onto a new path. Sometimes it's about realizing that the road you've been walking—with all its twists and pivots—was preparing you all along for a purpose you hadn't yet named.

My decades in tech were spent in high-stakes environments, leading project-focused teams with precision and clarity. I was expected to bring solutions; to manage deadlines, deliverables, and bottom lines; and to deliver transformational and breakthrough products. But even then, I found myself evolving, becoming most energized not by solving technical problems but by building capacity and empowering other people to solve them.

That's when something began to shift. I realized I wasn't just leading and managing people—I was coaching and mentoring them. I was helping them reconnect with clarity and align their decisions with their identity. I wasn't doing it formally yet, but the foundation had already been laid.

From the outside, the shift from leading engineering project management teams to coaching may seem like a pivot. But to me, it felt like a return. While building project management offices across a number of corporations, the goals were communication, structure, and providing a service. Coaching taught me how to focus on the person. In both, the aim is alignment—whether it's between systems or within the self. And what I've discovered is that the tools aren't all that different. The frameworks I used in my technical career—systems, models, diagnostics, feedback loops—have all become tools I now apply to coaching people in their professional and personal growth. What's changed is the context. The data isn't from customer usage or KPIs; it's from measuring professional and personal goals, dreams, and happiness in metrics. The results aren't product launches—they're breakthroughs.

CHAPTER TWO

THE ACCIDENTAL COACH

I never set out to become a coach.

Coaching didn't appear in some grand vision or business plan. It found me—organically, unexpectedly—and gradually took root in the most natural way possible. Looking back, I now understand that the seeds of this work were planted many years ago in my career, when I led high-performing teams, guided senior leaders, and developed talent in fast-paced, high-stakes environments.

In those roles, I was doing more than just managing. I was listening. Guiding. Challenging. Uplifting. Helping others unlock their potential became something I found not just rewarding but essential to who I am. It wasn't just a leadership skill. It was a calling.

People sought me out—not because I hung out a shingle but because they observed and saw something they wanted. They saw help getting to where they wanted to be because I had been where they wanted to go, and now, I am where they want to be. They came to me for perspective, clarity, encouragement, and hard truths. At first, I didn't think much of it. But over time, I recognized the pattern: I wasn't just advising and mentoring—I was coaching. And I was built for it.

My Coaching Palette: What I Bring to the Table

When people ask me what kind of coach I am, the short answer is: I'm an executive leadership coach who blends decades of tech and Silicon Valley rigor with deep, human-centered coaching. I help highly motivated, purpose-driven leaders design, build, and launch their next big chapter with clarity, confidence, and strategic intention. My style is structured yet intuitive—equal parts vision, challenge, framework, neuroscience, and heart.

It's a configurable, adaptive approach to each client and situation. I don't offer rigid programs. I bring the Design-Build-Launch framework and apply it to whatever the moment calls for—whether that's executive leadership, career transitions, entrepreneurial ventures, or personal transformation.

Figure 1: The Design-Build-Launch Framework

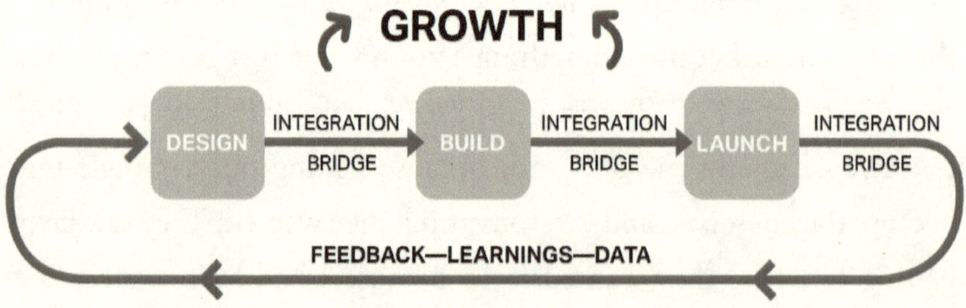

The Cloudberry Coaching Method

Coaching is a continuation of my previous work, not a departure from it. I'm taking everything I learned about leadership, coaching, systems, people, structure, and flow, and applying it to help others create groundbreaking breakthroughs in their lives, reengineer their approach, and launch into their next big chapter.

COACHING AS PROJECT MANAGEMENT AND PRODUCT DEVELOPMENT

The Cloudberry Coaching Method (CCM) emerges from a simple principle: Build around the person's actual needs and dreams.

In tech, we never built something because we could and then tried to create a market and find clients. It was the other way around. We built things because someone needed them, and we designed those solutions to exceed expectations. The CCM operates the same way: Need comes first; framework and process adapt accordingly.

This matters because one-size-fits-all models just don't fit everyone. They hand the same materials to every client regardless of background, goals, or working style. It's efficient for the coach, but it reduces human complexity to a checklist.

The CCM is modular and customizable. Some clients thrive with written reflection and structured worksheets. Others process aloud and prefer real-time dialogue. Some love metrics and want to score decisions using weighted frameworks. The method flexes to fit the person, not the other way around.

CHAPTER THREE

DESIGN, BUILD, LAUNCH

The CCM is a framework that moves from concept to execution with clarity, iteration, and momentum. Design. Build. Launch.

This process creates structure for transformation. People—like products and projects—need vision and systems to grow. Whether someone wants to move up into a more ambitious role, change careers, retire, improve relationships, start a business, or align their lives with what fulfills them, the CCM offers a clear, replicable path forward.

Phase 1: Design

All transformation starts with intention. Design is where bold clarity begins.

The Design phase grounds you in your *foundation*—mission, vision, values, and purpose. You then move into *ideation*, exploring identity, possibilities, ambitions, and direction. Next, define your *scope*—range, boundaries, constraints, and capacity that support traction.

Assess your *environment*—context, conditions, energy, and friction points. Then, acknowledge *challenges*—risks, reflex, and resilience.

Finally, identify your *team*—roles, responsibilities, dynamics, and connection.

Design is the architecture of your next chapter, where deep reflection meets bold direction.

Phase 2: Build

Build turns clarity into capability.

You begin with *tools*—developing systems, skills, routines, and metrics for progress. You then identify *resources*—time, energy, knowledge, and capital that align with your goals.

You develop your *roadmap* with milestones, dependencies, sequencing, and priorities for adaptation. Then, focus on *confidence* with mindset, skill, rehearsal, and readiness to match your vision. Next, you *prototype* through testing, validation, feedback, and agility. Lastly, focus on *stress* via pressure, load, performance, and recovery.

This is where traction forms and clarity deepens through practice.

Phase 3: Launch

Launch is where your work becomes visible and integrated into the world.

You start with *boldness*—ensuring that nerve, permission, courage, and leap are addressed. Then, focus on *execution*—presence, activation, pilot, and rollout. Establish *support* systems with mentors, allies, systems, and accountability that hold momentum. *Scale* through leverage, efficiency, sustainability, and growth. Then, *learning* through reflection, data, discernment, and synthesis. Finally, *evolution* involves rest, renewal, resilience, and transformation.

This isn't a onetime event—it's the beginning of how you'll lead, create, and grow.

The Living Loop

The CCM is cyclical. Design → Build → Launch. It's something you do repeatedly, at every level of your life.

Whether you're planning your next career move, navigating relationships, building healthier habits, or preparing to lead more effectively, this structure holds. It takes the mystery out of movement and gives you a process you can trust.

You don't need to change your entire life overnight. You just need to design the next step, build support for it, and launch it into motion.

Each cycle builds on the previous one, creating compound growth rather than starting over. You're not reinventing yourself—you're evolving into your next iteration.

The rest takes care of itself.

Why Neuroscience Belongs in This Coaching Method

One of my favorite questions, in career, in life, and in coaching, is: How does this work?

When I first experienced the power of coaching, I didn't just want to accept it at face value. I needed to understand it. And I've found that many of my clients are just as curious and feel the same way. They want to know: Why does coaching work so well? What's happening during powerful coaching moments? How do presence, questions, and visioning create change? Why does it happen in the order you've laid out?

This is where neuroscience enters the picture.

The breakthrough research by Richard Boyatzis and Anthony Jack at Case Western Reserve University provides compelling evidence for what I've observed in practice: Coaching works because it aligns with how we're wired to grow. Their studies revealed that coaching with compassion activates entirely different brain networks than problem-focused, compliance-based coaching.[1]

When coaches help clients connect with their vision and possibilities, several powerful things happen. The brain's default mode network engages, supporting openness to new ideas and social connection. Motivation centers activate. Stress response systems calm. The visual cortex lights up, enabling true "visioning." Most importantly, people become more receptive to learning and change.

This research validates that starting with vision and possibility creates the neurological conditions for sustainable transformation. When we begin with Design—grounding in values, exploring possibilities, setting direction—we're not just being systematic. We're working with the brain's natural architecture for growth.

The alternative approach—jumping straight into problem-solving and compliance—triggers stress responses that make change harder. It closes down openness and creativity while increasing defensiveness.

The more I've studied how we process stress, emotion, change, and learning, the clearer it's become: Systematic coaching succeeds because it honors how transformation works. We have two primary

---

1 Anthony I. Jack, Richard E. Boyatzis, Masud S. Khawaja, Angela M. Passarelli, and Regina L. Leckie, "Visioning in the Brain: An fMRI Study of Inspirational Coaching and Mentoring," *Social Neuroscience* 8, no. 4 (2013): 369–84, doi.org/10.1080/17470919.2013.808259.

networks in our brains. Neuroscientists call them the task-positive network (TPN) and the default mode network (DMN). The TPN supports focus, analysis, and execution. The DMN supports reflection, meaning-making, social connection, and vision. Sustainable growth doesn't come from living in one or the other—it comes from learning how to shift between them with intention.

That's why you'll find what I'm calling Neuroscience Nuggets throughout the Design-Build-Launch methodology that follows. Each nugget offers science-backed insight into what's happening under the surface. They're not just interesting facts. They're evidence that systematic, compassion-based coaching isn't just effective—it's neurologically intelligent.

If you're someone who wants to know how things work, consider these nuggets your user manual for change. They're a core part of what makes the CCM powerful and built to last.

Now let's explore the complete Design-Build-Launch framework that puts this science into practice.

What I've outlined here—Design, Build, Launch—is straightforward. After years of refinement with hundreds of clients, I've discovered that sustainable transformation requires this approach. Each phase contains multiple critical components that determine whether change sticks or fades.

What follows is the complete CCM—the comprehensive framework that transforms these three phases into an eighteen-pillar system for creating lasting change.

DESIGN

WHERE BOLD CLARITY BEGINS

Everything starts here. Before you build, before you step into the arena, before you launch, you design.

Design is where alignment starts to meet intention. It's the foundation for your next big chapter, your next business, your next career move, your next life adventure, or your retirement. Design creates clarity that makes action purposeful and momentum sustainable.

In the CCM, Design is deliberate exploration that connects you to the deeper truths driving your next big chapter. Your transformation. Who are you becoming? What anchors guide every decision? What vision calls you forward? And what is the why connecting it all together? You start with alignment.

Design requires rigorous honesty. You clarify what you want to create and who you need to become to build it. What you design shapes what you build, and what you build determines what you launch.

Design creates clarity and purposeful flexibility for the unknowns you will encounter along the path forward.

Design unfolds across six pillars, modular elements that act as building blocks for clarity and direction.

Foundation grounds in mission, vision, values, and purpose.

Ideation expands through identity, possibilities, ambitions, and direction.

Scope focuses with range, boundaries, constraints, and capacity.

Environment frames through context, conditions, energy, and friction.

Challenges are mitigated by assessing risks, reflex, and resilience.

Team supports through roles, responsibilities, dynamics, and connection.

Each pillar builds on what came before and prepares you for what comes next. Design creates the framework everything else depends on.

If Design feels slower than jumping straight into action, good. This phase is more about sustainability and less about short-term fixes. You're building the architecture now to move faster later. Without clarity here, your Build may lack focus, and your Launch will miss the mark.

Figure 2: The Design Phase

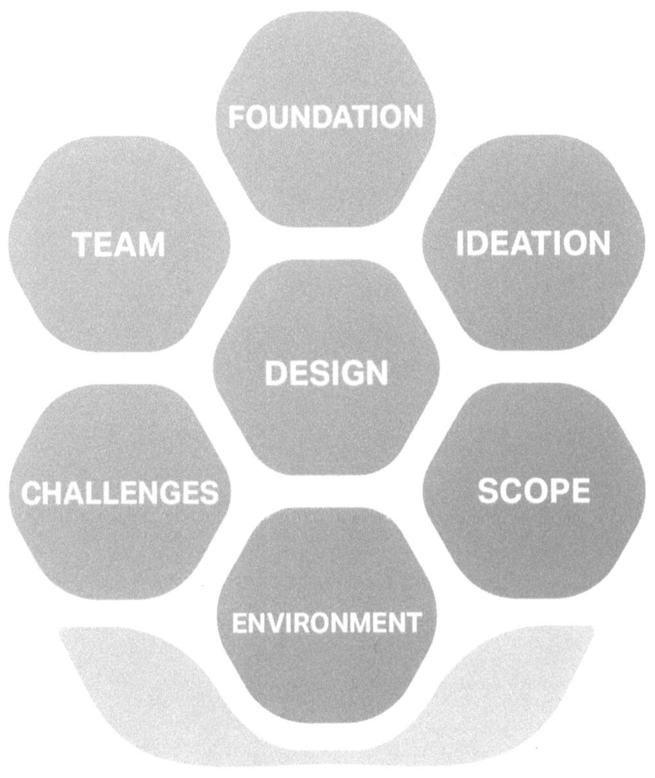

CHAPTER FOUR

FOUNDATION

Mission | Vision | Values | Purpose

Foundation is the inner architecture. It defines what you stand for, where you're going, why it matters, and how you choose to show up. It's where transformation begins—not with action but with clarity. Before you can design what's next, you need to understand what's already true about who you are, what you value, where you're headed, and—maybe most importantly—who you're becoming.

Foundation work is about making conscious choices about the principles, vision, and identity that will guide your decisions going forward. It's the difference between reacting to life and designing it.

Mission is *what* you're here to create.

Vision is *where* you're directed.

Values are *what* anchors you—your core operating system.

Purpose is *why* it all matters.

When your values, vision, mission, and purpose are aligned with what you build and launch, you become unstoppable. Decision-making becomes simpler. You have clear criteria for what fits and what doesn't, and you become more aligned with your "true north."

It's practical groundwork. The clearer your foundation, the more focused your actions become. The more focused your actions, the greater your energy and impact. The greater your impact, the more momentum you build toward the life you actually want.

Strong foundations accelerate progress. That's backed by science. When you're clear about who you are and where you're going, tactical decisions become more obvious. Energy flows toward what matters instead of scattering across competing priorities. Change feels natural rather than forced because it's aligned with your core.

Foundation answers the essential questions: Who are you? What matters most to you? Where are you going? What are you building?

For now, let's focus less on the how.

NEUROSCIENCE NUGGET

Purpose-driven goals activate motivation and meaning networks in the brain, increasing commitment and persistence when a challenge arises. When values and purpose align with action, the nervous system interprets effort as meaningful rather than threatening, reducing stress and increasing resilience. Mission and vision aren't slogans—they are neurological stabilizers.[2]

---

2 Richard E. Boyatzis and Anthony I. Jack, "The Neuroscience of Coaching," *Consulting Psychology Journal: Practice and Research* 70, no. 1 (2018): 11–27, doi.org/10.1037/cpb0000095; Lisa Feldman Barrett, *Seven and a Half Lessons About the Brain* (Houghton Mifflin Harcourt, 2020).

Mission

Your mission is what you're here to create, what you're building toward right now—not what you *think* you should be doing but what you're actively creating in your life today, this week, this month.

Mission is the bridge between your purpose and your vision. While your vision may stretch far into the horizon, your mission brings it into focus, turning aspiration into action as we progress through the Design-Build-Launch framework.

A well-defined mission starts to create traction. It directs your energy and shapes your daily decisions. It gives structure to how you spend your time, what you say yes to, and where you place your focus. Without it, even the most exciting vision can float untethered. With it, momentum becomes measurable.

Missions are living things. They evolve as you grow, shift as your environment changes, and refine with experience. But at any moment, be able to name what you're building and why it matters.

Vision

Vision is your destination, the compelling future you're building toward. In the CCM, vision is a bold, expansive look at what you're creating, not just in your work but in your life. Though vision sometimes gets confused with strategic planning—the how—they're different. Vision defines the targeted endpoint at the end of the trail, while strategy defines how to get there.

Vision aligns your focus and engagement in the present and reminds you what you're walking toward when the trail disappears or the fog rolls in.

Vision operates differently than ambitions and goals. Goals are finite; you achieve them and move on. Vision is infinite; it evolves as you grow, always pulling you toward a bigger version of yourself and your impact. It's the answer to this question: When you imagine your dream future, where are you and what does your life look like?

When clearly defined, vision becomes a filter. It helps you say yes to opportunities that support it and no to distractions that don't. It transforms scattered effort into focused momentum. It turns daily choices into building blocks of something meaningful.

The most powerful visions feel both inspiring and inevitable—big enough to stretch you, specific enough to guide you, and authentic enough to sustain you through the inevitable obstacles ahead.

Values

In the CCM, values are your personal operating system—the things that anchor you during calm waters and during change when the waves are rough. They're not goals to be reached—they're principles to be honored. They govern your decisions, including how you respond to feedback, navigate conflict, set boundaries, and lead under pressure.

When you're not aligned with your values, it shows up as ineffective friction. Burnout. Second-guessing. You're adrift, like a stranger in your own story.

Values are your best and strongest decision-making filters. When opportunity knocks, your values help you discern between what looks good and what actually fits. When pressure mounts, they anchor you to what matters most. When others try to pull you off course, they become your compass back to center.

The most powerful values are lived, not simply items on a list. Values often overlap and are in play simultaneously. Like a bittersweet experience. Like being fulfilled by both connections and boundaries. Like boldness with humility. They show up in how you spend your time, where you invest your energy, and what you're willing to say no to.

Purpose

Purpose is your why—the reason you're here, the reason you do what you do, and the reason it matters. It's the throughline that connects everything.

In the CCM, purpose is the deepest layer of your foundation. It's what gives weight to your mission, direction to your vision, and meaning to your values. Without clarity of purpose, you can achieve goals and still feel empty. With it, even the smallest steps carry significance.

Purpose is already there, woven into your story, your strengths, your passions, and the impact you naturally create. The work is to name it, claim it, and let it guide you forward.

When you're connected to your purpose, decisions become easier. You stop chasing every opportunity and start choosing the ones that align. You stop performing just for approval or validation (though, to seek this is to be human) and start building for impact.

Purpose doesn't have to be grand or world-changing. It just has to be true. Some people are here to create change. Some are here to heal. Some are here to build. Some are here to lead, to teach, to connect, to create, to inspire. When you seek your why, the how and the what become clearer.

Coaching Questions

MISSION

- What are you actively building toward in this chapter of your life?
- If your next chapter had a clear deliverable, what would it be?

VISION

- When you imagine your dream life one, three, and five years from now, what does it look like?
- What vision are you afraid to say out loud but can't ignore?

VALUES

- What truly matters to you? Family? Service? Love? Nature? Integrity?
- If someone watched how you spent last week, what values would they see? Ambition? Connection? Fun? Balance? Hard work?
- What principles anchor you during the rough times? Courage? Resilience? Faith? Groundedness? Community?

PURPOSE

- What do you feel called to do in this world?
- What themes keep repeating throughout your life?

CHAPTER FIVE

IDEATION

Identity | Possibilities | Ambitions | Direction

Ideation is where creativity meets constraint. After establishing your foundation, you need to generate the specific possibilities that will bridge where you are to where you want to be. This is strategic imagination.

Effective ideation finds the sweet spot: bold enough to excite you, grounded enough to pursue. It balances expansive thinking with practical application, ensuring your ideas can actually move from possibility to reality.

This phase combines two distinct but complementary processes. First, you expand what's imaginable, exploring possibilities without immediate judgment. Ask "what if" questions and follow interesting threads wherever they lead. Give yourself permission to consider. Then, you move on to ambitions, choosing what to pursue from the possibilities you've generated. Finally, you set direction, channeling your identity, possibilities, and ambitions into creating a path you can actually walk.

The magic happens in the tension between. Pure possibility without direction becomes escapism, floating with too much freedom and too little process and framework. Pure direction without possibility risks becoming rigid limitation without broader meaning. But when you hold both simultaneously, you unlock the focus and the creative problem-solving that transform visions into reality.

Ideation reveals that you have more options than you thought and clearer preferences than you realized. It's where breakthrough solutions emerge, not from grinding harder on old approaches but from leaning into your strengths and discovering entirely new ways to think about the challenge.

NEUROSCIENCE NUGGET

Envisioning your future self uses the same neural systems as remembering your past, making imagined possibilities neurologically real enough to influence behavior. Ambition grows when the brain can "pre-experience" a possible future. When possibility is constrained by fear or old identity stories, the brain limits action. Ideation expands the mental landscape that the nervous system believes is possible.[3]

Identity

Identity is who you believe yourself to be and who you give yourself permission to become. In the CCM, identity shapes what feels possible, what actions feel natural, and what goals feel achievable. When your inner story supports your outer ambitions, momentum flows more easily into groundbreaking new areas.

---

3 Boyatzis and Jack, "The Neuroscience of Coaching"; Moheb Costandi, *Neuroplasticity* (The MIT Press, 2016).

Identity operates as the foundation for behavior. When you see yourself as a leader, leadership actions feel authentic. When you see yourself as courageous, bold, creative, and thriving, new ideas flow more naturally. When you believe you're capable of growth, challenges become opportunities rather than threats.

Real change happens at the identity level, when how you see yourself aligns with how you want to live. This isn't about pretending to be someone you're not. It's about expanding who you already are and stepping into a more integrated, powerful version of yourself.

Identity work means consciously choosing the stories you tell about who you are and what you're capable of. It means embracing possibilities you may have previously overlooked and allowing yourself, giving yourself permission (and relying less on permission from others), to grow into the person your vision requires.

Coaching Questions

- Who do you need to become to realize your vision?
- If you fully owned your narrative, without the need to ask anyone for permission, how would you show up differently?

Possibilities

Possibilities are the full horizon of what could exist. Ambitions are the possibilities you choose to pursue. Before you plan, you must imagine. Possibility is what breaks you out of conditioned patterns and invites you into new realms of potential. In the Design phase, you honor the power of expansive thinking, generating options without prematurely judging them as right or wrong, as good or bad.

Possibility work is about creating space for "what if" questions. Step into wonder, curiosity, and play. Follow sparks. Give airtime to the voice inside that says there's more available to you.

We often operate within artificial constraints—assumptions about what's possible based on past experience or inherited beliefs. Possibility thinking challenges those boundaries. It asks: What if the limitations I've accepted aren't actually real? What if there are options I haven't considered? What if I'm thinking too small?

This isn't fantasy or wishful thinking. It's strategic imagination. It's expanding the menu of options before you choose what to order. The broader your sense of what's possible, the more creative your solutions become. The more creative your solutions, the more breakthrough potential you unlock.

For many clients, this is where growth begins—not by solving problems (yet) but by expanding what's imaginable. Sometimes the answer isn't better execution of the same old strategy. Sometimes it's discovering a completely different way to be.

Coaching Questions

- What's a possibility you haven't let yourself consider?
- Where are you settling when you could be exploring?

- If constraints disappeared tomorrow, what would you pursue?
- What idea keeps whispering to you no matter how often you dismiss it?

Ambitions

In the CCM, ambition is the forward pull, chosen from possibilities. Ambitions inform the goals that stretch you into growth, creativity, and action. Ambitions are about where you find the most engagement and feel fully alive. They're the gateway to creating goals that make you just nervous enough to feel alive when you say them out loud.

Ambitions act like gravitational force that gives structure to your motivation. They pull you toward becoming someone new. The best ambitions sit just beyond your current skill set or network, but they're not fantasy. They require a stretch, and sometimes a gamble.

When you set a bold, meaningful ambition, you begin the work of becoming the person who can realize it. Your brain starts scanning for opportunities you previously missed. Your network expands as you seek out people who can help. Your skills develop because they have to.

Your body knows ambition before your mind can articulate it. Research shows the vagus nerve sends roughly 80 percent of its signals from body to brain—meaning physical sensations often arrive first. This is awareness—the first step in transformation. When an ambition genuinely aligns with who you are, you might feel expansion in your chest, energy in your limbs, or a sense of curiosity you can't yet explain. When it's misaligned, your body contracts—shoulders tighten, breath shortens, gut clenches. Learning to read these signals is part of designing with clarity.

Ambitions also reveal what's possible. They force you to question assumptions about your limitations and capacity. They challenge the stories you've been telling about what you can and can't do. They make you uncomfortable in the best possible way—the discomfort of growth rather than the discomfort of staying stuck.

The magic isn't in achieving every ambition you set. The magic is in who you become while pursuing them. The juice really is found in the journey.

That's the heart of the CCM: aligning your internal development with the external vision you're stepping into.

Coaching Questions

- What's an ambition that scares you and excites you in equal measure?
- If you knew you couldn't fail, what would you go after?
- What ambition is quietly calling your name right now?
- What would need to change about you for that ambition to become inevitable?

Direction

After you name what's possible and choose your ambitions, you need a sense of direction. In the CCM, direction is not a rigid plan. It's a trajectory, a way of moving forward with intention while staying flexible as reality unfolds.

Vision defines where you're ultimately headed. Direction defines how you begin. Vision is the mountain. Direction is the path you start walking. Many people have a powerful vision but remain stuck because they never decide which way to move first. Direction turns aspiration into motion.

Direction requires synthesis. You look at your identity, your ambitions, your values, your possibilities, and ask: Given all of this, what makes the most sense right now? What is calling me forward? What wants to happen next?

Direction does not require complete clarity and full certainty. It requires commitment to the next step. You choose a few steps of action, begin moving, and let momentum reveal what you could not see from the starting line. As you go, your experience gives you more data, and direction evolves with you. The fog begins to lift—not on its own but because you're taking action.

A strong sense of direction reduces noise, busywork, and emotional friction. Decision-making becomes easier because every choice is measured against where you're headed. It releases you from trying to do everything and focuses your energy on what actually moves you forward.

It is about alignment, momentum, and the courage to begin.

Coaching Question

- What's the next set of small movements—action steps—that would create real momentum right now?

___

___

___

___

___

___

___

___

___

___

CHAPTER SIX

SCOPE

Range | Boundaries | Constraints | Capacity

Scope creates the container: what's in, what's out, what fits your vision and your current season, and what your energy and resources can sustainably hold. It's where possibility meets the reality of life and work.

You can do anything, but you can't do everything. Scope is the art of defining what you'll pursue and what you'll let go. In the CCM, scope is about focusing your energy so your dreams can actually happen; it's not about limiting your potential.

Without scope, even the most inspiring vision becomes overwhelming. You chase everything and build little or, even worse, nothing. You say yes to opportunities (people pleasing, anyone?) that don't serve you and then wonder why you're exhausted.

Scope creates the container that makes transformation possible. Ever had curiosity kill your productivity? Maybe run down a few too many riveting online rabbit holes?

This pillar explores four essential dimensions. Range defines how far and wide your focus extends. Boundaries establish the edges that protect your energy and intention. Constraints reveal the productive limits around focus and creativity. Capacity examines how much you can realistically hold and sustain over time.

Together, these elements help you design what's achievable without sacrificing what's meaningful. Scope isn't about playing small. It's about playing smart and building something feasible instead of chasing every possibility.

NEUROSCIENCE NUGGET

Scope protects your prefrontal cortex from cognitive overload. When everything matters, the brain loses the ability to prioritize, and threat networks take over. Clear constraints reduce uncertainty, narrow the decision space, and increase executive function—allowing you to focus deeply within healthy limits.[4]

Range

Range is about defining what's in and what's out. It transforms strategy into daily action—small, meaningful, and actionable bites—by creating alignment between your choices and your bigger vision.

"What's in" represents your core commitments: the projects, relationships, and activities that directly support your mission and vision. These are your priorities, the areas where you'll invest your best energy and attention. They get your protected time, resources, and focus. They produce your return on investment.

---

4 Daniel Kahneman, *Thinking, Fast and Slow* (Farrar, Straus and Giroux, 2011); David Rock, *Your Brain at Work: Strategies for Overcoming Distraction, Regaining Focus, and Working Smarter All Day Long* (Harper Business, 2009).

"What's out" creates equally important clarity: the opportunities, requests, and activities you'll gracefully decline or delegate. These include good ideas that aren't great fits, requests that pull you away from priorities, and activities that consume more energy than they generate.

The key insight: Saying yes to everything means saying yes to nothing meaningful. Attractive maybes dilute your focus and fragment your energy. Ranges with clearly defined borders help create decision-making speed and confidence.

When opportunity arrives, you can quickly assess whether it aligns with your range of focus. If it does, you engage fully. If it doesn't, you pass and redirect energy toward what matters most.

Boundaries

Boundaries are operating agreements that define how you live and work, what you're available for, and what you need to be your best and do your best work. Clear boundaries channel your energy toward what matters most while helping others understand how to work with you effectively.

Boundaries are the more specific guide rails that exist within your range of effort toward work, family members, friends, fun, finances, projects, and wellness, for example. What are the upper and lower limits you will tolerate? These limits let others know how to successfully collaborate with you. They create clarity by establishing expectations up front. They protect your ability to show up fully for what you've committed to by preventing energy drain and resentment from overcommitting—the worst kind of poison for a relationship.

Boundaries operate at multiple levels: time boundaries (when you're available), energy boundaries (what work you're able to take on), emotional boundaries (how you handle difficult relationships), and values boundaries (what principles guide your decisions).

The strongest boundaries are proactive. You design them into your systems from the beginning rather than scrambling to create limits when you're already overwhelmed. You build some margin into your schedule, create clear communication protocols, and establish core priorities that protect your most important work.

The best boundaries evolve with your priorities. They require regular attention and occasional adjustment as your goals and circumstances change. This maintenance keeps them effective and relevant to your current big chapter.

Constraints

Constraints channel innovation by providing focus and direction. When you understand your limitations, you can work with them strategically to create breakthrough solutions.

Every meaningful project and relationship operates within constraints: time, budget, energy, skill, satisfaction, risk, market conditions, and quality, to name just a few. The opportunity lies in using them strategically. The most innovative creators work brilliantly within real-world limitations rather than waiting for perfect conditions. After all, this is how the real world operates.

In a world full of distractions and endless options, constraints demand focus and making tough decisions. A breakthrough sometimes comes from working creatively with what you have rather than waiting for better conditions, more resources, or more time to magically appear.

The key is distinguishing between chosen constraints and out-of-your-control circumstances. Chosen constraints—such as deadlines or budgets—create productive focus. Given circumstances—such as market conditions or life stage—call for you to adapt over time.

Working skillfully within constraints means maximizing what you can control while accepting what you can't change. It means finding opportunity within limitations and building momentum with available resources.

Capacity

Capacity is about knowing your limits and honoring them. It's the honest assessment of how much you can realistically hold—emotionally, mentally, physically, and practically—without breaking down or burning out.

Understanding capacity means recognizing that you're not infinite. Your energy is renewable but not unlimited. Your attention has bandwidth. Your time is fixed. Your nervous system needs recovery. Ignoring these realities doesn't make you more productive; it makes your way of life unsustainable.

Capacity isn't static. It expands and contracts based on season, circumstance, stress, support, and health. What you could handle last year might overwhelm you now. What feels impossible today might become manageable with the right systems and support.

The most effective leaders and creators aren't those who are always pushing the hardest; they're those who understand their capacity and design their lives accordingly. They build margin into their schedules. They protect recovery time. They say no to preserve yes for what matters most. They say yes to more time to ensure a quality product.

Capacity work requires brutal honesty. It means acknowledging when you're at your edge and choosing rest over hustle. It means recognizing that doing less often creates more impact than doing everything poorly. It means building a life that's ambitious *and* sustainable, not just one or the other.

Coaching Questions

- Where would clearer boundaries instantly create more energy and focus?
- What can you realistically hold right now—and what needs to be released?

CHAPTER SEVEN

ENVIRONMENT

Context | Conditions | Energy | Friction

Smart growth works with environmental forces rather than against them. When your environment supports your dreams and ambitions, your growth becomes much more natural.

Environmental design operates on four interconnected levels: context, conditions, energy, and friction. Your context is the external circumstances you're navigating. Your conditions are the structures and systems shaping your daily reality. Your energy reflects what fuels and drains you. Your friction reveals where resistance, both good and bad, consistently shows up. Each level provides data about how to make choices and how to structure sustainable change.

You might underestimate how powerfully your environment drives behavior. A cluttered desk raises cognitive load. A stressed morning primes the nervous system for reactivity. Nonstop digital news and notifications fracture attention. The places you live, the cultures you work in, and even the friends and family you spend time with nudge you toward or away from your goals. Context isn't neutral—it's always shaping you.

The goal is to intentionally design your environment so it pulls you toward your intentions rather than away from them. Small environmental changes often produce outsized results because they create meaningful healthy patterns, requiring less decision-making.

Environmental design is practical systems work. It's moving the gym clothes next to your bed, scheduling focused work during your peak energy hours, and surrounding yourself with people who support your growth. It's engineering success into your daily life.

NEUROSCIENCE NUGGET

Your environment determines how much of your brain is available for learning and high-level thinking. Supportive conditions reduce threat activation and free cognitive resources for creativity, problem-solving, and emotional regulation. Environments filled with friction, uncertainty, or chronic distraction trigger the brain's survival networks, shrinking cognitive flexibility and emotional capacity. When conditions feel safe and aligned, the nervous system interprets effort as manageable, and performance rises.[5]

Context

Context is your current reality—the season you're in and the external demands and constraints you're working within. Honoring your current context is how you begin to create change that sticks.

---

5 Richard E. Boyatzis, Melvin L. Smith, and Ellen Van Oosten, *Helping People Change: Coaching with Compassion for Lifelong Learning and Growth* (Harvard Business Review Press, 2019).

Context includes everything that shapes your daily experience: work demands, family responsibilities, health status, financial situation, geographic location, relationship dynamics, and life stage. Think of these factors as design parameters rather than obstacles.

The executive who travels constantly needs different systems than someone with a predictable routine. The parent of young children designs differently than the empty nester. The person managing a health challenge approaches goals differently than someone in peak physical condition.

Context-aware design doesn't mean settling for less—it means being strategic about timing, pacing, and resource allocation. Sometimes context requires you to slow down before you can speed up. Sometimes it means focusing on maintenance before pursuing growth. Sometimes it means addressing one area of life before tackling another.

The most successful growth works in harmony with life context rather than fighting against it, when you find ways to build momentum within current constraints rather than waiting for perfect conditions that may never come.

Conditions

Conditions are the climate in which growth happens—or doesn't. In the CCM, conditions represent the external and internal environment that shapes how you operate day to day. They include the tangible and intangible factors that either support or strain progress toward your next big chapter.

Conditions reflect intentional choices to create an environment that nurtures clarity, creativity, and consistency. Your brain is sensitive to context. When conditions are misaligned with your goals and your values, your nervous system perceives constant threat, which impairs decision-making and drains energy. When conditions support your direction, even simple actions feel easier because your environment is working with you, not against you.

Conditions operate on multiple levels. Structural conditions include your physical setup, time systems, and workflow design—the practical scaffolding that determines whether your habits hold. Relational conditions involve the people around you: mentors, peers, family, and colleagues who either fuel or drain your focus. Cultural conditions include the broader expectations and norms you're navigating: workplace culture, community values, or societal pressures that can either inspire or inhibit your growth.

EXAMPLES OF CONDITIONS IN ACTION

Relational condition that supports: "My boss is supportive of career changes." This provides emotional safety and practical flexibility to take calculated risks and explore new directions.

Cultural condition that supports: "My workplace rewards risk-taking." This creates psychological safety to innovate, experiment, and pursue ambitious goals without fear of punishment.

Structural condition that constrains: "I work sixty-hour weeks with no flexibility for professional development." This makes it difficult to prototype new routines, invest in skill development, or create space for strategic thinking.

Designing your next chapter means honestly assessing which conditions are working for you and which need to change—or which environment you need to change. It's about aligning your external world with your internal goals by calibrating every factor: where you work, when you work, your daily schedule, who you bring into your inner circle, your workspace, how you reframe your mindset, and how and where you engage with others.

The goal is to build supportive conditions, not necessarily perfect ones—conditions that make alignment easier, recovery faster, and progress sustainable. Because the right conditions don't just enable performance—they protect it.

Energy

Everything is energy. And energy impacts everything. Awareness of what fuels you—and what drains you—is one of the most practical steps you can take toward sustainable progress.

Energy is about how you relate to the people, projects, environments, and activities that either give you life or drain it away. Are you living in fear and shame and anger—emotions that tank your energy—or in a space of bravery, cooperation with others, and joy in possibility? Does your environment create what fuels you, or are you constantly fighting?

Energy sources are highly individual. Some people are energized by collaboration, others by solitude. Some thrive on variety, others on routine. Some are fueled by intellectual challenges, others by creative expression. The key is knowing your specific profile and designing your life accordingly.

Energy management *and* time management win every time, because your energy follows your focus. When you prioritize energy, everything else becomes more effective.

Energy management is about intentional investment. You want to direct your energy toward activities that align with your values and advance your mission while protecting reserves for what matters most.

Some energy expenditure is necessary and worthwhile—the key is making conscious choices about where your energy goes.

Friction

Friction is where intention meets reality—and reality pushes back. It's the resistance, the slowdown, the patterns that persist. Friction is data—information pointing toward what needs attention.

Friction shows up everywhere: the project that keeps lagging, the routine you abandon, the creative work that stalls, the difficult conversation you keep avoiding, the boundary you can't seem to maintain. Each friction point reveals something important about misalignment, hidden fears, competing priorities, or systems that no longer serve you.

And friction isn't always bad. Pressure refines. Heat transforms. Diamonds, pearls, muscles, innovation, resilience—even great books—are forged through friction. Some friction strengthens you, builds capacity, increases clarity, and prepares you for what comes next. Other friction drains you, signals misalignment, or points toward necessary change. The skill is knowing the difference.

Rather than powering through friction or avoiding it entirely, get curious about it. What is it trying to tell you? What needs to shift? Maybe your approach needs refinement, the timing requires patience, or there's an underlying issue waiting to be addressed.

Friction management distinguishes between productive friction, which signals you're stretching and growing, and counter-productive friction, which signals misalignment. Some resistance is worth working through, while some is wisdom pointing toward a better path.

Coaching Questions

- How can you work within your current reality instead of waiting for it to change?
- What conditions help you do your best work—and how can you create more of them?
- Where is friction showing up, and what might it be trying to tell you?

CHAPTER EIGHT

CHALLENGES

Risks | Reflex | Resilience

Challenges are inevitable—external risks, internal patterns, stress responses, and the capacity to adapt, recover, and grow stronger. Every meaningful change involves navigating all three of the following: the risks you'll face, the reflexes that emerge under pressure, and the resilience you'll need to move forward. Rather than hoping challenges won't appear, you need to be prepared to skillfully work with them.

In the CCM, challenges operate across interconnected elements. Risks are what you face—both the external domains that threaten progress and the internal patterns that derail momentum. Reflex is how you react—the automatic responses and default behaviors that emerge before conscious thought. Resilience is how you recover and adapt—your capacity to learn from setbacks and grow stronger through difficulty.

The goal is to anticipate and navigate challenges with awareness and skill, not necessarily to eliminate them. When you can name your risks, recognize your reflexes, and strengthen your resilience, challenges become design constraints that lead to stronger, more sustainable outcomes.

You can't mitigate what you don't name. This pillar is about building your challenge muscle to see clearly, respond wisely, and grow through whatever comes.

NEUROSCIENCE NUGGET

The brain is wired to treat uncertainty and risk as potential threats, triggering reflexive survival responses that shut down innovation, creativity, and long-term thinking. But when challenges are framed as learning opportunities instead of danger, the brain shifts into exploratory networks that increase cognitive flexibility, curiosity, and emotional regulation. Resilience isn't toughness—it's the neurobiological ability to recover, reengage, and reattempt after stress. Each time you face a challenge and adapt instead of retreat, you strengthen the neural pathways that make future uncertainty easier to navigate.[6]

Risks

Risks are the real and perceived threats to progress that influence your decisions and shape your path forward. In the CCM, risk isn't just external circumstance; it's an ecosystem that includes both the systemic challenges you'll encounter and the internal patterns that can derail progress from within.

Understanding your complete risk ecosystem means seeing both sides clearly. External risks are the tangible domains that create vulnerability during change: financial uncertainty, relational disrup-

---

6 Steve Magness, *Do Hard Things: Why We Get Resilience Wrong and the Surprising Science of Real Toughness* (HarperOne, 2022); David Rock and Linda J. Page, *Coaching with the Brain in Mind: Foundations for Practice* (Wiley, 2009).

tion, reputational exposure, strategic miscalculation, and operational breakdown. Internal risks are the psychological patterns that intensify under pressure and uncertainty: fear of failure, perfectionism, avoidance, control, and the risk of being truly seen.

What makes risk particularly challenging is how external and internal factors interact. Financial pressure amplifies perfectionism. Relational uncertainty triggers avoidance. Strategic (the how) risk activates control patterns. The systems outside you and the patterns inside you create a feedback loop that either supports or hinders forward movement.

The first step in navigating risk isn't eliminating it—it's developing the capacity to see it clearly, assess it accurately, and prepare strategically rather than react defensively.

EXTERNAL RISKS: COMMON DOMAINS

Financial risk: the economic vulnerability that comes with transition—income gaps, investment costs, reduced earning potential, or uncertainty about sustainable revenue. Financial risk isn't just about having enough money. It's about how long you can afford uncertainty while building something new and, most importantly, how you relate to money overall. Money is about more than dollars; it's emotional—tied to memories, identity, and what matters most to you.

Relational risk: the potential disruption to important relationships during significant change. Some connections will evolve and others may end, and you'll need to build new relationships aligned with your direction. The question isn't whether relationships will shift—it's which ones matter enough to protect and how you'll navigate the transitions.

Reputational risk: the exposure that comes with visibility, change, or failure. When you step into something new, you risk being seen, judged, misunderstood, or criticized. Reputational risk includes both the fear of losing credibility and the discomfort of being more visible than you've been before.

Operational risk: the challenges of execution—capacity constraints, skill gaps, resource limitations, or system failures. Operational risk is about whether you can deliver on what you're building, maintain quality under pressure, and sustain momentum through the inevitable setbacks.

INTERNAL RISKS: COMMON PATTERNS

Fear of failure: the paralyzing worry that you'll fall short, disappoint others, or prove your doubts right. This pattern shows up as procrastination, over-preparation, analysis paralysis, or avoiding situations where failure is possible. It's not necessarily about being careful—it's about awareness and choosing to not let fear dictate your choices.

Perfectionism: the belief that anything less than flawless is unacceptable. Perfectionism delays action, unrealistically inflates standards, and creates impossible expectations. It masquerades as excellence but prevents progress by making "good" or even "great" feel like failure. This is different from striving for a perfect product or a perfect end outcome.

Avoidance: the tendency to sidestep discomfort, difficult conversations, or challenging situations. Avoidance can take the form of procrastination, distraction, rationalization, or simply choosing easier but lesser paths. It protects you from short-term discomfort while creating long-term stagnation.

Control: the need to manage every variable, minimize uncertainty, and maintain predictability. Control patterns emerge when you continually try to force outcomes rather than influence conditions. They show up as micromanagement, rigidity, or resistance to collaboration and delegation.

Risk of being seen: the fear of visibility, exposure, or authenticity. This pattern keeps you playing small, dimming your voice, or hiding behind credentials and accomplishments. It's the risk that if people really see you, they'll find you lacking—so you avoid being fully visible.

THE RISK ECOSYSTEM

External and internal risks don't operate independently—they create feedback loops that either amplify threat or build capacity. Financial pressure can trigger perfectionism and control. Relational uncertainty can activate avoidance. Reputational risk can intensify fear of failure and the impulse to stay hidden.

Skillfully navigating risk means seeing the whole ecosystem: the external domains that require strategic preparation and the internal patterns that need focused management. When you can name both sides, you can design around them rather than being controlled by them.

Coaching Questions

- Which external risk domain feels most threatening to your next chapter, and what specific preparation would help you navigate it?
- Which internal risk pattern shows up most consistently when you're under pressure or building momentum?

- How do your external risks and internal patterns interact to either amplify threat or support growth?
- What factors would need to feel safer—internally or externally—for you to move forward despite the risks?
- What's one risk you've been avoiding naming that needs to be acknowledged and addressed?

Reflex

Reflex is how you react, or predict what will happen, before you think—the automatic responses, default behaviors, and unconscious patterns that emerge under pressure, uncertainty, or stress. In the CCM, reflex isn't about willpower or discipline; it's about understanding how the brain predicts and responds based on past experience and then building the capacity to create a new pathway when it no longer serves you.

Dr. Lisa Feldman Barrett's research reveals a critical insight: Your brain doesn't merely react to the world—it predicts what will happen based on past patterns and then acts on those predictions.

This means your reflexes and emotions aren't just responses to current circumstances; they're inherited patterns shaped by previous experiences, cultural conditioning, and learned survival strategies. The fight-flight-freeze-fix-fawn-fine spectrum isn't a flaw—it's how your nervous system learned to protect you.

The challenge is that reflexes optimized for past contexts often become liabilities in new situations. The defensive posture that protected you in a toxic workplace may sabotage collaboration in a healthy team. The perfectionism that earned recognition in school may prevent you from shipping work that's good enough. The control patterns that helped you manage chaos may limit your ability to delegate and scale.

Reflex work isn't about eliminating automatic responses—it's about developing awareness so you can recognize patterns as they emerge and choose whether to follow them or interrupt them. It's about expanding the space that exists between stimulus and response so that conscious choice becomes possible. And the more you focus on it, the more this space expands.

PREDICTION: HOW YOUR BRAIN CREATES REALITY

Your brain is a prediction machine. It constantly generates best guesses about what will happen next based on past experience, then filters incoming information through those predictions. This means you're not experiencing reality directly—you're experiencing your brain's prediction of reality, updated moment by moment as new data arrives. Emotions play a central role in this process, serving as part of the brain's predictive system rather than as reactions that come afterward.

Reflexive patterns emerge from deeply ingrained predictions. If your nervous system learned that visibility leads to criticism, you'll reflexively minimize your presence. If past experience taught you that vulnerability invites rejection, you'll automatically armor up. If your system predicts that mistakes equal failure, you'll default to perfectionism or avoidance.

These predictions happen below conscious awareness, which is why reflexes feel so automatic. By the time you notice the pattern, you're already reacting. Awareness begins with recognizing that what emotionally feels like truth is often just prediction—and predictions can be updated.

PATTERN AWARENESS: RECOGNIZING THE REFLEX

Pattern awareness is the practice of noticing your reflexive responses without immediately acting on them. It's gaining awareness of the defensive thought before it becomes defensive speech. It's recognizing the urge to withdraw before you actually isolate. It's seeing the perfectionist standard rising before it derails progress. These reflexes are often driven by unconscious predictions your brain is making to keep you safe—based on past experience, not present reality.

This ability comes from curiosity and practice. In this realm, willpower is highly overrated. You begin to notice the physical sensations that precede reflexive action: the tightness in your chest before you snap, the sinking feeling before you avoid, the surge of energy before you overcommit. These body signals are your early warning system, revealing patterns before they fully activate.

The goal is to avoid judging reflexes as good or bad and, instead, to recognize them as information. Each reflex points to something your system is trying to protect. When you can observe patterns with curiosity rather than criticism, you create the possibility of choosing different responses.

The key is starting with awareness, not perfection. You won't interrupt every reflex, and that isn't the goal. The goal is building the capacity to recognize patterns and choose differently when it matters most.

Resilience

Resilience is how you recover and grow stronger through challenge—not just bouncing back but becoming more capable. In the CCM, resilience isn't just about toughing it out or pushing through pain. It's about building the capacity to learn from setbacks and adapt in ways that make you stronger.

There's an important distinction here. Endurance is about survival—pushing through without breaking. Adaptability is about flexibility—adjusting when conditions change. True resilience is about transformation—becoming stronger because of the challenge. This is what separates sustainable high performance from burnout.

Resilience bridges from automatic reaction to intentional response. After the initial reaction comes the critical question: What now? How do you process what happened, create the learning, and integrate it in ways that strengthen your capacity for what's next?

Here's the key insight: Resilience isn't built during the challenge—it's built in the space after, through reflection, rest, and restoration. The most resilient people aren't those who never struggle; they're those who've developed practices for recovering well and learning deeply.

Recovery is the foundation of resilience. Without restoration, challenge accumulates as chronic stress, depleting your nervous system and impairing your ability to think clearly, regulate emotions, and access creativity. Physical recovery includes sleep, nutrition, movement, and rest—the basics that get sacrificed first when pressure increases, precisely when they matter most. Emotional recovery means processing what you've experienced rather than suppressing it. Mental recovery means giving your brain a break from constant problem-solving and decision-making.

Recovery isn't optional maintenance—it's how you prevent depletion from becoming damage. The goal is awareness of healthy—and unhealthy—levels of stress and to build the capacity to recover fully so you can meet the next challenge with renewed energy and capability rather than running on empty.

Coaching Questions

- Which risk—internal or external—feels most real right now, and what would make you feel safer to move forward?
- When pressure rises, what automatic reflex shows up (fight, flight, freeze, fix, fawn, fine), and how could you name it, claim it, and own it?

CHAPTER NINE

TEAM

Roles | Responsibilities | Dynamics | Connection

Build your support system intentionally—the people who believe in you, build with you, challenge you, and walk beside you.

Every transformation needs a team: your allies, partners, and thought leaders. This pillar helps you design how that team functions by defining roles, clarifying responsibilities, shaping healthy dynamics, and maintaining genuine connection.

Transformation isn't a solo journey. The people you surround yourself with—allies who believe in you, partners who build with you, and thought leaders who expand your thinking—shape both your process and your outcomes. Your team doesn't need to be large—in fact, smaller is often better—but it needs to be intentional.

Conscious relationship design during major transitions is often overlooked. Going it alone, whether from habit, fear of being a burden, or the myth of self-reliance, makes change harder than it needs to be. Isolation during transformation is counterproductive.

The right relationships provide perspective when you're too close to see clearly, encouragement when doubt creeps in, and accountability when momentum wanes.

Building your team requires being specific about what you need and strategic about who can provide it. Some people offer emotional support, others bring expertise, and still others provide networks or resources. The key is matching the right people to the right needs rather than expecting any single relationship to meet every need.

The goal is to curate relationships that challenge you to grow, support you through difficulty, and celebrate your progress along the way. Whether you're an executive launching a new initiative, an entrepreneur building a business, or someone navigating a major life transition, you need your people, and you need to design how that ecosystem functions.

Because we can't do this work alone. And we're not meant to.

NEUROSCIENCE NUGGET

Effective teams require more than clarity of responsibilities—they require psychological safety. When people feel safe to contribute, ask questions, and disagree without fear, the brain stays in learning and problem-solving mode. When safety breaks down, the brain shifts into self-protection, narrowing perspective and reducing collaboration. Strong team dynamics activate social bonding and reward networks that increase trust, creativity, and collective intelligence. Alignment and connection are not soft skills—they are neurological infrastructure for high-performing teams.[7]

7 Rock and Page, *Coaching with the Brain in Mind*; Boyatzis et al., *Helping People Change*.

Roles

Roles define the types of support you need in your ecosystem as you navigate transformation. These aren't rigid categories or boxes to check—they're different kinds of support that matter at different moments. One person can serve multiple roles, and often your most valuable relationships do exactly that. Your coach might be an ally, collaborator, and thought leader all at once. Your partner might champion your work while also being your closest ally. A mentor might challenge your thinking while opening doors you couldn't access alone.

Understanding these roles helps you recognize what kind of support you need in any given moment and who naturally provides it. The goal isn't to collect people who fit one category—it's to build a complete ecosystem where these types of support are present, whether from one person or many.

Your support ecosystem includes a few primary role types, each serving distinct purposes.

Allies are the people who believe in you, especially when you're struggling to believe in yourself. They see your potential and offer unwavering emotional support and encouragement. They help you take risks and stay committed through difficult phases. You may have more allies than you realize. Some are cheering quietly from the sidelines, waiting for permission to step closer. Others are friends who would gladly support your growth if they knew what you needed.

Champions are the people who actively advocate for you and your work. They don't just believe in you—they tell others about you. They open doors, make introductions, recommend you for opportunities, and speak up on your behalf when you're not in the room. Champions see your potential and use their influence to help you advance. They might be mentors, sponsors, former colleagues, or influential connections who believe in what you're building and want to help you succeed.

Collaborators are the people you build with—advisors, co-creators, and those who bring complementary skills, perspectives, or networks to what you're creating. Great collaborations are built on mutual benefit and clarity about what each person brings to the relationship. You might work with someone whose strengths balance your gaps, whose network opens doors you couldn't access alone, or whose experience helps you navigate unfamiliar territory. Collaborators can be formal business relationships, peers exploring similar transitions, mentors offering guidance, or friends who become thought partners and accountability allies for specific goals.

Thought leaders serve as intellectual partners who expand your thinking and provide models for what's possible. These are coaches, authors, researchers, practitioners, and thinkers whose work influences your perspective, challenges your old thinking, or offers different frameworks that organize your experience. At times, they help you name what you've felt but couldn't articulate and provide language and structure for what you're building.

Understanding these roles prevents the common mistake of expecting one person to meet all of your needs or feeling disappointed when someone excels in one area but can't help in another. When you know what kind of support you need and who naturally provides it, you can build a complete ecosystem rather than over-relying on any single relationship. And you can recognize when one person—such as a great coach, champion, or mentor—serves multiple roles beautifully, which is often when the deepest transformation happens.

Responsibilities

Responsibilities define how relationships work—what you need, what you're offering, and how both people show up authentically. It's about clarity that creates trust and prevents the resentment that builds when expectations stay unspoken.

The best relationships involve generosity. When you're clear about what you need and what you can give, relationships feel sustainable rather than draining. This requires honest conversations about capacity, boundaries, and what each person can reasonably expect. It means being willing to both ask for help and receive it well, while also showing up for others when they need you.

Responsibility clarity prevents common pitfalls during transformation. It stops you from over-relying on people who can't sustain the weight you're placing on them. It helps you avoid guilt and feeling like a burden when you need extra support. It protects against one-sided dynamics where you're always taking or always giving without balance.

Being clear about responsibilities also means recognizing when support needs to be professional rather than personal. Some needs are best met by coaches, mentors, consultants, or other paid professionals who have both the expertise and the appropriate boundaries to provide sustained support. Expecting friends or family to serve functions better suited to professionals can unnecessarily strain relationships.

Sustainable support systems are built on explicit clarity about what's needed, what's possible, and how both people will know if something needs to shift. This might feel vulnerable initially, but clarity creates safety. When people know what's expected and what they can count on, relationships deepen rather than fracture under pressure.

Dynamics

Dynamics describe how you actually interact with your team—the quality of communication, the patterns of feedback, the cadence of engagement, and the foundation of trust that makes healthy interaction possible. Good dynamics don't happen automatically. They require intention, attention, and ongoing cultivation.

Trust is the foundation of functional dynamics. Without psychological safety, people can't be honest about challenges, admit mistakes, or take risks in front of each other. Trust develops through reliability, transparency, and demonstrated care over time. It's built through following through on commitments, being honest about limitations, showing up consistently, and responding to vulnerability with respect rather than judgment.

The best dynamics balance challenge and support. Your team should feel safe enough to be honest when you're off track, stuck in unhelpful patterns, or avoiding necessary action. But honesty only works if it's delivered with genuine care and belief in your capacity. Dynamics become toxic when challenge feels like criticism without care or when support enables stagnation rather than encouraging growth.

Healthy dynamics also require clear communication about how feedback will be given and received. Some people prefer direct, immediate input. Others need time to process before discussing challenges. Some thrive on frequent check-ins, while others need space between interactions. Understanding your own preferences and those of your team members prevents disconnection and strengthens connection.

Dynamics aren't static. As your transformation progresses, what you need from relationships will shift. Early stages might require more encouragement and brainstorming. Middle phases may need accountability and problem-solving. Later stages might focus on integration and celebration. Good dynamics adapt to what the moment requires rather than remaining rigidly stuck in one mode.

Connection

Connection is what makes your team sustainable rather than transactional. It's the genuine bond, the sense of being known and valued, and the ongoing cultivation of relationships that matter. In a culture increasingly defined by loneliness, in which the US Surgeon General has declared isolation a public health epidemic, intentional connection isn't optional. It's essential.

Loneliness doesn't just feel bad—it impairs cognitive function, weakens immune response, and significantly increases health risks. During transformation, when uncertainty already strains your system, isolation amplifies stress and undermines resilience. Connection, by contrast, activates systems that reduce stress, enhance learning, and increase your capacity to navigate difficulty.

Connection requires ongoing tending, not just initial setup. Relationships atrophy without attention. The mentor who was invaluable six months ago may drift away if you haven't stayed in touch. The friend who offered support might not know you still need it unless you reach out. Connection work means regular check-ins, updates on progress, expressions of gratitude, and genuine curiosity about others' lives beyond what they can do for you.

Connection also means vulnerability. Letting people see your actual struggles, not just the polished version of your journey, deepens relationships and invites more meaningful support. The paradox of transformation is that the moments when you most need connection are often when you're most tempted to isolate. Shame, fear of being a burden, or the belief that you should handle everything alone pushes people away precisely when they could be most helpful.

Building and maintaining connection isn't selfish—it's strategic. Your capacity to create meaningful change is directly linked to the quality of relationships supporting you. The executive who tries to transform their organization while personally isolated will burn out. The entrepreneur who builds alone will miss critical blind spots. The person navigating life transition without genuine connection will struggle unnecessarily.

Connection is what transforms a collection of individuals into an actual team. It's what makes support sustainable, feedback land well, and celebration feel meaningful. In a world that makes connection harder than ever, choosing to build and tend genuine relationships becomes an act of both wisdom and courage.

Coaching Questions

- Who genuinely believes in you and wants to see you win—and have you invited them in?
- What support do you actually need right now, and have you clearly asked for it?
- Where are you isolating when connection would help you move further, faster?

Integration Bridge: The Gateway from Design to Build

WHERE CLARITY BECOMES CAPABILITY

You've designed with intention. You clarified your mission, vision, values, and purpose. You explored identity and ambition. You defined scope, examined your environment, identified challenges, and assembled your team.

Now you stand at the threshold where clarity must become capability. This is the moment when your aspirations, dreams, and goals transform into planning and building—when possibility becomes progress.

THE SHIFT

In Design, you created clarity. In Build, you will create structure and capability.

You will develop the systems, skills, routines, resources, confidence, and prototypes that make execution sustainable. Build turns insight into infrastructure. You're not executing a plan—yet.

WHAT THIS BRIDGE CHECKS

Before stepping into Build, confirm three things:

1. Coherence

   Your six Design pillars align—they reinforce rather than contradict each other. Your scope matches your capacity. Your environment supports your ambitions. Your team covers critical roles. Your challenges are manageable given your resources and resilience.

If there's misalignment, this is when you catch it. Better to redesign now than discover the gaps mid-build.

2. Commitment

You're not exploring anymore—you're choosing. Build requires focus. You can't build everything at once. What are you committing to build first? What are you putting on the back burner or deferring?

Commitment isn't forever. It's for this phase. But without it, Build becomes scattered rather than deliberate development.

3. Readiness

Practical readiness, not perfection, is essential. Do you have enough clarity to start? Enough resources to begin? Enough support to sustain effort? You don't need all the answers. You need enough foundation to take the first step.

When these three conditions are true, you're ready enough—not certain, but ready.

FROM PLANNING TO PRACTICING

In the CCM, Build is where you stop theorizing and start testing reality. You develop systems that actually work for you. You build skills through deliberate practice. You create routines that match your energy patterns. You prototype ideas in low-stakes environments before high-stakes launches.

Build is where you experiment. You'll discover that plans that looked good on paper don't work in practice. Your initial roadmap will need adjustment. Your confidence will waver. Your stress tolerance will be tested.

That's learning. Build is where you develop capability by confronting what you don't yet know how to do.

THE COACHING OF THIS MOMENT

This is when resistance shows up disguised as perfectionism:

"I need more clarity before I start."

"Let me refine the design one more time."

"I should do more research first."

"Maybe I'm not ready yet."

Design can become an infinite loop if you let it. At some point, more designing doesn't create more clarity—it creates procrastination.

Build requires choosing small decisions over certainty. You grow into capability by practicing, not by preparing endlessly.

WHAT CHANGES IN BUILD

You shift:

- from exploring possibilities to developing capabilities,
- from asking What if? to testing what actually works,
- from clarity about vision to confidence through action, and
- from design decisions to operational systems.

Your work starts to become tangible.

This is where momentum begins—not in perfect planning but in imperfect practice.

IF YOU FEEL HESITATION HERE

Good! That's normal. Build asks you to encounter reality—which won't cooperate perfectly with your plans.

The discomfort is a sign that you're growing.

THE BRIDGE STATEMENT

You've done the clarity work. You know what you're building and why it matters. It's time to develop the capability to make it real.

Welcome to Build.

BUILD

WHERE CLARITY BECOMES CREATION

Design gave you clarity. Build gives you momentum.

Build is where your foundation stops being theoretical and starts becoming real. You're not launching yet—you're constructing the infrastructure that will make Launch successful. In Build, you assemble the tools, routines, skills, and support systems that turn intention into capability.

This phase is about progress that prepares you for execution. It's laying down stable scaffolding, developing the skill to act with confidence, and stress-testing your ideas on a small scale before they meet the real world, building confidence along the way. Prototype, not rollout, lives here.

Some people skip Build. They jump from Design to Launch and wonder why momentum collapses, why burnout hits, or why everything feels chaotic. Build prevents that. It creates readiness. It turns clarity and capability into structure so Launch isn't a leap of faith from the edge—it's a continuation of prepared action.

Build operates across six essential pillars: tools, resources, roadmap, confidence, prototype, and stress. Each one strengthens the foundation so future execution is sustainable, strategic, and aligned.

Figure 3: The Build Phase

CHAPTER TEN

TOOLS

Systems | Skills | Routines | Metrics

Start building with what you have and stop waiting for perfect conditions.

Tools are the difference between intention and impact. In the CCM, tools operate across the following critical elements: the systems you're implementing, the skills you're developing, the routines you're establishing, and the metrics that keep you on track. This isn't about collecting more productivity apps or learning every possible technique. It's about assembling exactly what you need to turn today's bite-sized, achievable actions into tomorrow's results.

The best tools amplify your natural strengths while covering your blind spots. A morning routine that energizes someone else might drain you. A project management system that works for your colleague might overwhelm your brain. Your tools need to fit your wiring, not fight it.

The key is finding your sweet spot: the right amount of structure without overwhelming complexity. Smart tool-building is iterative. You start with the minimum viable toolkit—basic skills, simple systems, reliable routines—and then upgrade as you grow. The task management approach that works when you're managing three priorities becomes inadequate when you're coordinating multiple projects. Your tools should evolve with your ambition.

The goal is to create capability for what matters most. When your essential capabilities are reliable and your fundamental routines are automatic, the reward is freed up cognitive and emotional bandwidth for creativity, focus, and your best work.

NEUROSCIENCE NUGGET

The brain builds capability through repetition and feedback. Every time you perform a skill—whether it's a strategic routine, a new workflow, or a daily habit—neurons that fire together wire together. Deliberate practice strengthens the neural pathways responsible for focus, execution, and decision-making. Over time, actions that once required effort become automatic, freeing up cognitive resources for creativity and problem-solving. Metrics reinforce this process by giving real feedback the brain can learn from, accelerating adaptation and skill growth.[8]

8 Norman Doidge, *The Brain That Changes Itself: Stories of Personal Triumph from the Frontiers of Brain Science* (Penguin, 2007); James E. Zull, *The Art of Changing the Brain: Enriching the Practice of Teaching by Exploring the Biology of Learning* (Stylus, 2002).

Systems

Systems are the repeatable structures that organize your life, work, priorities, and information. They're how you capture ideas, track commitments, manage projects, and ensure nothing critical falls through the cracks. Good systems create reliability. They mean you don't have to remember everything because you've designed ways to remember what matters.

Systems range from simple to sophisticated. A weekly review process is a system. A project management workflow is a system. The way you organize files, handle emails, track finances, or manage your calendar—all systems. What matters isn't complexity but consistency. The system you actually use beats the perfect system you abandon.

The best systems are invisible until you need them. They run in the background, creating order without demanding constant attention. But when you need to find information, make a decision, or coordinate action, the system provides exactly what you need, when you need it. This reliability reduces cognitive load and decision fatigue, preserving mental energy for higher-value work.

Systems also create accountability and visibility. When you can see what's committed, what's progressing, and what's stuck, you can make better decisions about where to focus attention. Metrics emerge naturally from good systems—as feedback that helps you understand what's working and what needs adjustment.

Let pain points guide system development rather than building infrastructure you don't yet need.

Skills

Skills are your edge—the capabilities you're developing to support the future you're building. In Build, skills are strengths, becoming the practical abilities that turn your vision into something you can actually execute.

Some skills are technical: mastering software, learning methodologies, and building marketing expertise. Others are human behavioral skills that help you adjust, pivot, and operate under changing or stressful conditions, such as communicating under pressure, creatively solving problems, and regulating emotion during uncertainty. Both skill sets matter because Build requires capability. Intention alone isn't enough.

The most valuable skills compound the more they are used. Facilitation makes you a stronger leader. Systems thinking makes you a stronger strategist. Emotional intelligence makes you stronger everywhere. These aren't just tools for work—they're upgrades to how you operate in life.

Let's prioritize transferable skills—the ones that serve multiple contexts and grow more powerful with use. The ability to synthesize information, stay calm under pressure, or navigate difficult conversations will serve you in every room you enter.

Skills grow through deliberate practice, not passive exposure. Consuming information isn't mastery. Skill is built in action—with feedback, reflection, repetition, and meaningful stretch. Build asks: What do you need to get better at *now* for the future you're creating?

Routines

Routines are your daily and weekly rhythms that maintain momentum without requiring constant decision-making. They create consistency in an unpredictable world and ensure important activities happen regardless of how you feel on any given day.

The power of routines is in creating automatic progress toward what matters most. A morning routine that includes physical movement sets a foundation for energy all day. A weekly review routine ensures nothing important falls through the cracks. An evening routine creates a transition from work mode to personal time.

Design routines around your energy patterns and life context. If you're most creative in the morning, build routines that protect that time for your most important work. If you're managing young children, create routines that account for interrupted schedules and shifting priorities.

Start small and build gradually. A ten-minute morning routine you do consistently beats an elaborate hour-long routine you abandon after a week. Once simple routines become automatic, you can expand them or add new ones.

Metrics

Metrics are how you know if what you're building is working. They're the data points that tell you whether you're making progress, spinning your wheels, or heading in the wrong direction. Without metrics, you're operating on hope and intuition alone.

Good metrics are about creating feedback loops that inform future design decisions. Metrics answer questions such as: Is this approach effective? Are we moving toward the goal? What needs adjustment? They turn abstract aspirations into concrete evidence.

The key is choosing the right metrics—not everything that's measurable matters, and not everything that matters is easily measurable. Revenue is a metric. So is your energy level at the end of each day. Satisfaction is a metric. So is how often you're operating from your values versus your fears and frustrations; we know that metrics override fear.

Start with leading indicators—the behaviors and inputs you control—rather than only tracking lagging indicators such as outcomes. If your goal is a career transition, track conversations with people in your target field, not just job offers. If you're building a business, track outreach and pilot conversations, not just closed deals. If you're getting healthier, track steps taken per day. Leading indicators give you actionable data before outcomes crystallize.

Metrics should serve you. They're tools for learning and adjustment. When a metric reveals something isn't working, that's useful information and an opportunity to adjust.

Coaching Questions

- What tool or structure would remove friction and make your next steps easier?
- Where are you relying on memory or willpower when a system could carry the weight?
- What repeatable process could save you time, energy, or decision fatigue?

CHAPTER ELEVEN

RESOURCES

Time | Energy | Knowledge | Capital

Resources are how you use what you have—and how you shore up what you need. In Build, resource alignment becomes essential. Nobody has unlimited time, endless energy, or infinite knowledge. Smart resource management means making intentional choices about where your finite resources go and ensuring those choices serve your deeper purpose, not scattered urgency.

The reactive approach drains resources fast.
Time gets eaten by whatever screams loudest.
Energy gets poured into low-value tasks.
Knowledge gets collected instead of applied.
Money gets spent fearfully or impulsively.
Capacity stretches until something breaks.

Build flips the script.

You start allocating resources on purpose.

You design around values, mission, and goals.

You invest your time, energy, knowledge, and capital like the strategic assets they are.

You honor your capacity—not as a weakness but as the boundary that makes sustainable performance possible.

Smart resource management creates alignment between what you have and what you're trying to build. When your resources flow toward priorities instead of noise, progress stops feeling like a grind and starts feeling natural, steady, and sustainable.

NEUROSCIENCE NUGGET

Cognitive and emotional resources are finite. The brain draws from a shared energy budget for focus, self-control, learning, and decision-making. When too many demands pull from that budget, performance drops—not because of a lack of willpower but because the brain prioritizes conservation and survival. Protecting time, simplifying decisions, and reducing friction preserve neural resources for work that matters most, making progress more sustainable.[9]

Time

Time is your most nonrenewable resource. You can't create more of it, pause it, or borrow it from tomorrow. The question in Build isn't how busy you are—it's whether your time is fueling what matters. Productivity aimed in the wrong direction is just waste.

Time is architecture. How you shape it determines the quality of your work, your energy, your relationships, and your momentum

9 Barrett, *Seven and a Half Lessons*; Kahneman, *Thinking, Fast and Slow*.

toward your next chapter. Intentional time creates progress. Reactive time lets urgency swallow everything important.

Effective time allocation starts with clarity.

What are your nonnegotiables—work, family, health, commitments?

What time is left to build what's next?

What actually deserves your best focus, not just whatever attention is left at the end of the day?

Time also requires protection. Your calendar reflects your values—or exposes the gap between what you say matters and what you consistently act on. Build means intentionally blocking space for strategy, creativity, recovery, and the habits that strengthen you.

Time needs rhythm. Some days are for sprints, some for rest, some for learning, and some for execution. When every day is treated the same, especially a nonstop sprint, burnout becomes inevitable. Build invites honest design—time aligned to capacity, not fantasy.

The goal isn't to fill every minute. The goal is to invest your minutes where they count.

Energy

Energy is the fuel that powers Build. Cognitive energy for strategy. Emotional energy for hard conversations. Creative energy for innovation. Social energy for collaboration. Physical energy for sustained effort. You need all of it—and it has limits.

In the CCM, energy is a strategic resource. You design your Build around when you have what kind of energy, not around an idealized schedule that ignores your reality.

Energy comes from rhythm and recovery. You build patterns that protect capacity: batching similar tasks to reduce switching costs, honoring peak cognitive hours for deep work, creating transitions between different kinds of tasks, and treating recovery as essential, not indulgent.

Different phases require different energy. Design needs reflective, strategic energy. Build needs sustained focus. Launch needs visible, outward-facing energy. Knowing your phase helps you intentionally allocate your power.

Energy compounds or collapses based on alignment. Work connected to your purpose can energize you even when it's hard. Work that conflicts with your values drains you even when it's easy. Build means designing around what energizes you, not just what feels urgent.

Energy management is about sustainability. Invest your best energy where it matters, honor your real capacity, and protect the resources you need to reach Launch without burning out.

Knowledge

Knowledge is the intellectual capital that expands what's possible. It includes experience, frameworks that organize complexity, and expertise that accelerates progress. In Build, knowledge is about capability—not trivia.

Strategic learning starts with focus.

What gap is blocking your next move?

What expertise would unlock momentum?

What understanding would help you navigate complexity with more confidence?

Build asks you to learn through action—not just reading and consuming but testing ideas, trying things, making mistakes, and adjusting. This kind of learning becomes embodied. It sticks.

Depth matters more than volume.

Deep expertise in a few areas creates leverage; shallow knowledge in everything creates noise. Focus on what compounds and what transfers across contexts. Let your vision—not your curiosity alone—guide your learning.

And don't ignore the knowledge you already have.

Experience is data.

Data reduces fear and frustration.

Reflection turns it into wisdom.

Build means fully leveraging what you know, not assuming you're starting at zero.

Capital

Capital is the fuel that powers Build. Money matters—but so do relationships, credibility, trust, systems, and infrastructure. All forms of capital can be invested, depleted, or grown.

Financial clarity matters.

What does this phase actually cost?

What resources does sustainable execution require?

Where will investment create leverage?

What's worth paying for versus building yourself?

Smart investment isn't about spending—it's about multiplying capacity. The right tool, the right hire, or the right bit of expert help might cost money now, but it will save months of effort and accelerate momentum.

Nonfinancial capital matters just as much.

Relationships open doors.

Reputation creates trust.

Systems multiply output.

All require intentional investment—time, integrity, consistency, and follow-through.

Capital also requires honesty about runway. How long can you sustain this Build phase with the resources you have? What must be true—financially, relationally, and operationally—to reach Launch without breaking?

Build doesn't require recklessness.

It requires clarity and courage in how you deploy what you have.

Coaching Questions

- What do you need more of—and what will you do to get it?
- Where can you get support instead of trying to hold everything yourself?
- What resource is already available that you haven't been using?

CHAPTER TWELVE

ROADMAP

Milestones | Dependencies | Sequencing | Priorities

The future is a design challenge, not a problem. In Build, you seek less rigid planning and more flexibility. You need optional paths, smart contingencies, and decision filters that keep you on course when terrain shifts.

Scenario thinking maps possibilities—Plan A, Plan B, Plan Bold. Explore what could go wrong and what could go right—faster than expected. Build capacity to pivot with purpose rather than overcommit to one rigid route.

Contingency signals leadership maturity. You trust yourself to navigate complexity and ambiguity. Scenarios built in from the start transform setbacks into signals, not stop signs.

The CCM calls this anchored flexibility.

A complete roadmap operates across four dimensions: milestones mark meaningful progress, dependencies connect current reality to desired outcomes, sequencing determines execution order, and priorities maintain momentum when plans shift.

NEUROSCIENCE NUGGET

The brain is built for prediction. Creating a visible sequence of steps shifts processing into the prefrontal cortex, where planning, focus, and motivation live. Even small, measurable progress releases dopamine, reinforcing momentum and making future action easier.

Clarity calms the brain. Sequencing turns fear into forward movement.

A roadmap transforms "someday" into something the brain trusts.[10]

Milestones

Milestones are how you turn progress into something real. They're the proof you can point to—the small wins that show you're actually moving, not just thinking about moving. In Build, milestones create momentum you can feel. They give you something to celebrate, something to measure, and something to learn from.

Good milestones are specific and observable.

"Work on the website" is fog.

"Finalize the landing page and publish it by October 4th" is a milestone.

Milestones answer a simple question: How will you know this step is truly done?

They also protect you from the fantasy of progress—the illusion of being busy without building. When you define what success looks

10 Boyatzis and Jack, "Neuroscience of Coaching."

like, you create accountability and confidence. You stop guessing and start measuring.

The best milestones stretch you without breaking you. They are big enough to feel meaningful but small enough to finish this week, not someday.

Dependencies

Dependencies are the building blocks of execution. They reveal what has to happen first, what can happen later, and what's blocking momentum right now. When you understand dependencies, you stop pushing on the wrong things and start working in the right order.

Dependencies create sequence:

You launch after you build.

You build after you design.

You design to start the framework.

They also extend beyond tasks.

Sometimes the dependency is a conversation.

Sometimes it's funding.

Sometimes it's learning a skill instead of trying to muscle through without it.

Mapping dependencies shows you where you're actually stuck—not where you assumed you were stuck. And it reveals leverage points; a single bottleneck cleared can unlock ten downstream actions. One decision made, one approval granted, one skill learned, and momentum accelerates.

Dependencies are the architecture of progress.

Sequencing

Sequencing is the order in which things happen. Not everything can—or should—happen at once. Good sequencing creates momentum by stacking progress: Each step makes the next one easier. Strategic sequencing respects that one thing enables another.

Sometimes you need quick wins early on to build confidence before tackling bigger moves. Other times, the most important work is foundational—the part no one sees, but without it, everything collapses. The right sequence depends on your context, capacity, and constraints.

Sequencing also protects learning. When you place steps in a thoughtful order, each phase builds capability that compounds. You become more skilled, more confident, and more prepared for what comes next. Mis-sequencing often leads to overwhelm or stalled progress—not because the goal is wrong but because the order worked against you.

The best sequencing balances logic and strategy. Pure logic might say, "Do the hardest thing first," but if that destroys momentum, it's not strategic. Build sequencing considers both: what makes sense on paper and what will actually keep you moving.

Priorities

Priorities are the things that get your focused attention when you can't do everything at once. They're the filter that separates what matters most from what matters less. In Build, priorities are driven by alignment and impact—not urgency or guilt.

Real prioritization means making choices: what gets attention, what gets deferred, what gets delegated, and what gets dropped entirely. Clear priorities turn scattered effort into meaningful progress.

Priorities also evolve. What mattered a month ago may not be what matters now. Build requires priorities that stay flexible enough to adapt but anchored enough to keep you moving toward your vision.

A good prioritization framework brings clarity without rigidity. It helps you distinguish urgent from important, strategic from distracting, and momentum-building from time-burning. When priorities are clear, decision-making becomes faster, lighter, and far less exhausting.

Coaching Questions

- What are the next three intentional steps that can make this real?
- What milestone will prove you're moving forward, not just thinking about it?
- If progress had to be simple, what would you do first?

CHAPTER THIRTEEN

CONFIDENCE

Mindset | Skill | Rehearsal | Readiness

Confidence in Build has two sources: how you think about yourself and what you prove to yourself through action. You need both. Thought without action creates doubt. Action without belief creates unnecessary struggle. Build aligns the internal and the external so they reinforce each other.

Confidence grows through evidence. Every time you take a step that once felt intimidating and discover you can handle it, your nervous system updates its prediction of what's possible.

This isn't just mindset—it's embodied. Confidence registers in your body as calm breath, grounded posture, and steady hands. Self-doubt shows up as shallow breathing, tight shoulders, or a racing heart. Your body is constantly signaling whether it believes you're safe or threatened. Building confidence means teaching your nervous system, through repeated action, that this challenge is manageable.

What felt risky becomes manageable. What felt overwhelming becomes familiar. Competence builds through doing, not just planning.

Confidence also grows through alignment. When your inner narrative supports your actions, progress feels natural. When your story contradicts your effort, even simple things feel heavy. Build asks you to develop the mindset that matches the chapter you're stepping into—not the one you're leaving.

Confidence in Build shows up across four domains:

- Mindset: the beliefs that shape how you interpret effort, failure, and possibility
- Skill: capability earned through deliberate practice and repetition
- Rehearsal: practicing before performing, reducing threat, and increasing ease
- Readiness: knowing you've built enough structure and capacity to take the next step

NEUROSCIENCE NUGGET

Confidence is built through experience. The brain encodes confidence when action and outcome align repeatedly. Practice strengthens neural pathways, reducing the sense of threat and increasing predictability. Mental rehearsal activates many of the same neural networks as physical execution, priming the brain for competence before the real moment arrives. Confidence grows from exposure, not avoidance, and the nervous system learns "I can handle this" through repetition, not perfection.[11]

Mindset

Mindset is the internal narrative that shapes how you interpret challenges, setbacks, and possibilities—in other words, your attitude. It's the deeper story you tell yourself about what you're capable of and what's possible for you. In Build, mindset determines whether obstacles feel like proof of inadequacy or opportunities for learning. The same setback lands completely differently depending on the story you're telling.

Mindset work means examining the beliefs driving your behavior and asking whether they're serving your growth. If you believe "people like me don't do things like this," that belief will tank every action you take. If you believe "I'm learning how to do this," the same actions build capability.

Shifting mindset requires awareness first: What do you actually believe about yourself and your capacity? Then: Is that belief true or just familiar? And finally: What would you need to believe to move forward with courage instead of fear?

Skill

Skill-based confidence comes from demonstrated capability. It's the evidence you build, through repeated action, that you can actually do the thing—concrete proof accumulated through deliberate practice.

Build reverses the typical sequence. Action creates confidence. Each time you attempt something difficult and survive, you rewire

11 Zull, *The Art of Changing the Brain*; Boyatzis and Jack, "Neuroscience of Coaching."

your brain's threat assessment. The thing that felt impossible becomes achievable, then routine, then boring. That's skill development.

Skill confidence is domain-specific. Being confident in one area doesn't automatically transfer to another. A brilliant strategist might lack confidence in public speaking. A gifted creator might doubt their business acumen. Build means identifying which skills need development and systematically strengthening them through focused practice.

The confidence that comes from skill is durable because it's earned. You remember that you've already done it. That changes everything.

Rehearsal

Rehearsal is where ideas become muscle memory, where uncertainty becomes familiarity, and where you build confidence before stepping into real stakes. Rehearsal shrinks fear by replacing the unknown with experience.

Rehearsal can be mental, verbal, or physical. You can walk through a presentation out loud, draft an email before sending it, role-play a difficult conversation, or simulate a launch with a small test group. The goal isn't perfection—it's familiarity. When you've rehearsed, your brain recognizes the situation and responds with more calm, clarity, and control.

Rehearsal also reveals gaps. When you run the play, you discover what's missing, what needs refinement, and where you need support. That feedback loop strengthens confidence because you're not just hoping you can perform—you've practiced performing.

Great performers rehearse not because they're uncertain but because it sharpens their edge. Build uses rehearsal as a strategic tool to reduce cognitive load, calm the nervous system, and prepare your best self to show up when it matters.

Readiness

Readiness is the subtle certainty that you're prepared—not perfect but prepared. It's the sense that you've done the work, you've built capability, and you're as ready as you're going to be. Readiness doesn't eliminate nerves; it transforms them from paralyzing fear into productive energy.

Readiness comes from completion. You've clarified your thinking, built the skills, and rehearsed what you can control. There is peace in knowing you've prepared well, even if outcomes remain uncertain. You trust your foundation.

Readiness also requires releasing the illusion of total control. You'll never eliminate risk or guarantee success. At some point, preparation becomes procrastination wearing a perfectionist mask. Readiness is knowing when more prep won't meaningfully improve outcomes—and it's time to step forward.

The shift from "I'm not ready yet" to "I'm ready enough" is a mindset shift, not a logistical one. Build helps you separate real gaps from fear-based hesitation. When you're ready, you don't feel certainty about the result—you feel trust in your ability to navigate what comes.

Coaching Questions

- What belief about yourself needs to shift for this next chapter to work?
- What have you already proven you can do—and how can you build on that?

- What could you practice before it counts?
- Discomfort is a green light on the learning curve—what action does it point to?

CHAPTER FOURTEEN

PROTOTYPE

Testing | Validation | Feedback | Agility

Test small to learn big. You don't need to launch perfectly—you need to learn rapidly. In Build, prototyping is one of your most powerful tools for moving from theory to reality. It allows you to test ideas in real conditions with low risk and high insight. A prototype is a small, intentional experiment that brings your vision into the world one manageable test at a time.

A prototype might be a pilot workshop, a rewritten bio, a side-project soft launch, or a new morning routine. It's not about scale. It's about traction. Momentum doesn't come from thinking harder; it comes from trying over and over and over again.

Prototyping reduces perfectionism and over-planning. It shifts your mindset from "I have to get it right" to "I get to learn as I go." Every prototype generates real feedback that sharpens your next move and builds evidence about what actually works.

This is about taking intentional, low-stakes steps that validate direction, clarify value, and build confidence through action. When done well, prototyping reveals what works, what doesn't work, and what wants to evolve. You're not guessing anymore—you're gathering truth.

Prototype in Build operates across four dimensions: testing, validation, feedback, and agility.

NEUROSCIENCE NUGGET

The brain learns fastest through real-world feedback. When you test ideas in small, low-stakes environments, you trigger the brain's prediction-and-correction loop: You act, observe the outcome, and adjust. Each cycle strengthens neural pathways that improve accuracy, skill, and confidence. Mistakes aren't signs of failure—they are biological accelerators of learning. Neuroplasticity increases most when the brain encounters something unexpected and adapts, which is why prototyping and quick adjustment build capability far faster than planning alone.[12]

Testing

Testing means running small experiments to learn before you commit fully. A test is action designed to produce learning, not proof of perfection. Tests remove the pressure of permanent decisions and replace them with curiosity.

Good tests are specific, bounded, and built around clear questions. "I want to see if this works" is hope. "I'll run three client sessions using this new framework and track whether clarity increases" is a test. The question shapes the experiment. The experiment yields data. Data informs our next action.

---

12 Costandi, *Neuroplasticity*; Doidge, *The Brain That Changes Itself*.

Testing builds momentum by creating early wins. If the test fails, you learn. If it succeeds, you expand. Either way, you're moving forward with information instead of speculation.

The best tests are reversible. Try the routine for two weeks. Share the draft with five trusted readers. Low commitment, high learning. That's smart testing.

Validation

Validation checks whether what you're creating actually solves the problem you think it solves. It's the difference between building something and building something you truly need.

Validation is evidence-based. Encouragement isn't validation. Someone saying "great idea" is support. Someone paying for it is proof. Someone nodding is politeness. Someone changing behavior because of your work is impact.

True validation starts by defining what proof looks like. What outcome would demonstrate success? Increased engagement? Changed behavior? Specific feedback? Metrics prevent you from cherry-picking data that confirms what you already believe.

Validation protects your runway. Better to discover misalignment after a small pilot than after a full launch. Validation surfaces truth early, when adjustments are cheap—not after you're too invested to pivot.

Feedback

Feedback is the external inputs that improve your work. It reveals what isn't visible from inside your own perspective. Useful feedback shows you where clarity is landing, where confusion remains, and where opportunity exists.

Not all feedback is equal. Some reflects the giver's fears or preferences, not objective insight. The goal isn't to accept all feedback—it's to discern the kind that reveals truth worth acting on.

Good feedback is specific and actionable. "I don't like it" isn't useful. "The opening is strong, but the transition is unclear" points toward improvement.

Seeking feedback requires courage. You're letting people see your work before it's perfect. But early feedback prevents you from building the wrong thing beautifully. In prototyping, course-correction is a feature, not a failure.

Agility

Agility is the willingness to adapt based on what you learn. It means staying committed to the vision while remaining flexible about the path.

Agility requires letting go of sunk costs—time, money, or ego already invested in an approach that isn't working. Pivoting based on evidence is intelligence in action.

Agile prototyping builds feedback loops into the process: weekly check-ins, metrics reviews, and reflection on what is and isn't working. The faster you learn, the faster you can adapt.

Adaptation means adjusting the route. The strongest builders evolve their plans based on real-world signals while staying anchored to purpose. That's agility.

Coaching Questions

- What is the smallest version you can launch to learn something real?

- What hypothesis are you testing—and how will you know if it's working?
- What would you try if you didn't need it to be perfect?

CHAPTER FIFTEEN

STRESS

Pressure | Load | Performance | Recovery

Stress is part of ambitious work. The question isn't whether you'll experience stress during Build. The question is whether you'll navigate it intelligently. In Build, stress management means understanding how pressure affects your capacity, recognizing when load exceeds your threshold, optimizing performance under constraint, and building recovery into your rhythm so you can sustain effort over time.

Build requires distinguishing between productive stress that drives growth and destructive stress that impairs function. You need to know your edge and how to work near it without crossing into burnout.

Stress exists on a spectrum. Some pressure enhances performance; too much crushes it. The skill is learning to read your signals, adjust your load, and create conditions in which you can perform well without depleting yourself.

Strategic stress management means working intelligently with stress.

Stress in Build operates across four dimensions: pressure, load, performance, and recovery.

NEUROSCIENCE NUGGET

Your nervous system has a narrow window where stress enhances performance and a breaking point where it destroys it. Moderate pressure increases focus and motivation, but excessive stress floods the body with cortisol and adrenaline, shutting down prefrontal cortex function—the part of the brain responsible for problem-solving, emotional regulation, and good decisions. When load overwhelms capacity, the brain shifts into survival mode and performance drops. Recovery isn't optional—sleep, rest, and emotional decompression reset the nervous system and restore executive function.[13]

Pressure

Pressure is the force of demands, expectations, and deadlines. Some pressure is energizing—it creates urgency and focus. Too much pressure becomes overwhelming and triggers threat responses that impair your ability to think clearly and act effectively.

The relationship between pressure and performance follows an inverted U-curve. Too little pressure, and motivation drops. Optimal pressure puts you in your zone of peak performance. Excessive pressure degrades decision-making, emotional regulation, physical health, and relationships.

Working with pressure means knowing where your sweet spot is. What level of challenge brings out your best work? At what point

---

13 Magness, *Do Hard Things*; Barrett, *Seven and a Half Lessons*; Rock, *Your Brain at Work*.

does pressure start to break you down? Everyone's curve is different. Your job is to know yours.

Pressure compounds. One deadline might be fine. Multiple deadlines—layered with personal stress and no recovery—stack into overload. Managing pressure means managing the whole system, not just one demand at a time.

Load

Load is the total weight you're carrying—not just tasks but also emotional demands, mental complexity, and personal responsibilities. Your nervous system doesn't separate them. Stress from one area affects capacity in all areas.

Load includes visible commitments, such as meetings and deadlines, and invisible load, such as decision fatigue, unresolved conflict, or chronic worry. Everything draws from the same finite pool of cognitive and emotional resources.

Managing load requires honesty about what you're actually carrying. What's on your calendar? What's on your mind? What's been weighing on your heart? You can't manage load that you won't acknowledge.

Reducing load doesn't always mean doing less. Sometimes it means resolving what's been lingering, delegating, or creating systems that reduce friction. The goal is sustainable capacity, not maximum output.

Performance

Performance under stress means maintaining capability when conditions aren't ideal. It's executing when you're tired, solving problems under time pressure, and staying grounded when things feel chaotic.

Performance degrades under excessive stress. Cognitive flexibility narrows. Emotional regulation decreases. Decision-making becomes reactive instead of strategic. Recognizing the early signs helps you intervene before performance collapses.

Sustained performance comes from operating within your window of tolerance—the zone where you're challenged but not overwhelmed. Inside that window, stress enhances performance. Outside it, stress destroys performance. You expand that window through preparation, experience, and recovery.

Performance improves when challenges feel expected rather than shocking. Mental rehearsal, scenario planning, and building response routines help reduce threat response and increase confidence when pressure hits.

Recovery

Recovery is physiology. Your nervous system cannot operate at high intensity indefinitely without breaking down. Recovery restores cognitive capacity, emotional regulation, and physical energy. Without it, performance degrades and health suffers.

Recovery happens at multiple time scales: micro recovery between tasks, daily recovery through sleep and downtime, weekly recovery through genuine rest, and seasonal recovery through breaks and resets. All of it matters.

True recovery requires disengagement—physically stopping and mentally releasing. Taking a day off while mentally ruminating is not recovery. Recovery is permission to reset.

Build requires sustained effort that depletes resources. Strategic recovery ensures you have the clarity, stability, and energy required for Launch. The Design-Build-Launch framework only works when recovery is treated as infrastructure, not reward.

Coaching Questions

- Where is pressure sharpening you—and where is it starting to break you down?
- What are you carrying that you haven't fully acknowledged?
- What early warning signs tell you you're leaving your performance zone?
- What would real recovery—not just time off—look like for you right now?

Integration Bridge: From Build to Launch

This is where capability becomes contribution.

You've translated clarity into capability. You built systems you trust. You invested time, energy, knowledge, and capital with intention.

You prototyped, validated, adjusted, and developed confidence grounded in evidence—not hope.

Now, you stand at the threshold where the work leaves the workshop and enters the world.

This is the moment when internal alignment becomes external contribution.

THE SHIFT

In Design, you created clarity.

In Build, you created capacity.

In Launch, you will create impact.

Launching is the next step in learning.

The world becomes your testing ground.

Launch turns theory into traction.

WHAT THIS BRIDGE CHECKS

Before stepping into Launch, confirm three things:

Fit: Your prototype addressed a current, real need.

Capacity: Your systems, routines, and resources can sustainably carry the load—without pushing you into overwhelm, burnout, or collapse.

Clarity: You can explain what you're doing, why it matters, and who you're becoming—in one breath. Simplicity makes your work accessible.

When these three conditions are true, you're ready enough. Not perfect—ready.

THE COACHING OF THIS MOMENT

This is where fear becomes storyteller:

"Wait until you're more experienced."

"Fix just one more thing."

"Run one more test."

"Next month, when life is calmer …"

Perfection protects the ego. Launch protects the dream.

Nobody ever feels fully ready. You grow into readiness by acting before certainty arrives.

WHAT CHANGES IN LAUNCH

You shift:

- from assumption to evidence,
- from practice to presence, and
- from building the solution to delivering the value.

Your impact becomes measurable.

IF YOU FEEL TENSION HERE

Good! That's normal. It's a sign you're doing something meaningful.

Build gives you capability.

Launch demands courage.

And then—because this framework is alive, not linear—you learn, evolve, and loop forward again.

THE BRIDGE STATEMENT

You've done the work.

You've earned this moment.

It's time to step from preparation into contribution.

Welcome to Launch.

LAUNCH

STEP INTO THE ARENA AND BE SEEN

You've designed with clarity.

You've built with intention.

Now, you launch with courage.

Launch is where alignment meets action. It's the moment you commit—to your next chapter, to your presence, to the systems that will hold it, to the people who need what you offer, and to the parts of yourself that are finally ready to emerge.

But Launch is not a single event. In the CCM, Launch is a season—a stretch of deliberate movement that includes initiation, visibility, support, testing, transition, and sustainability. It is emotional and strategic, external and internal. It asks you to both let go and show up.

Launch requires courage because you're no longer creating in private—you're contributing in public. You're shifting from experimentation to delivery, from preparation to presence. What you built is now something others can see, respond to, benefit from, challenge, or celebrate.

This isn't about perfection. It's about contribution.

It's not about certainty. It's about readiness.

Launch is where your work stops living in your head and starts living in the world—where the theoretical becomes practical and where possibility becomes impact.

Launch isn't a single moment. It's a phase of sustained contribution. It requires boldness to begin, execution to deliver, support to sustain, scale to grow, learning to improve, and evolution to transform. Each pillar builds on what came before and prepares you for what comes next. This is where your next big chapter stops being hypothetical and starts being real.

Figure 4: The Launch Phase

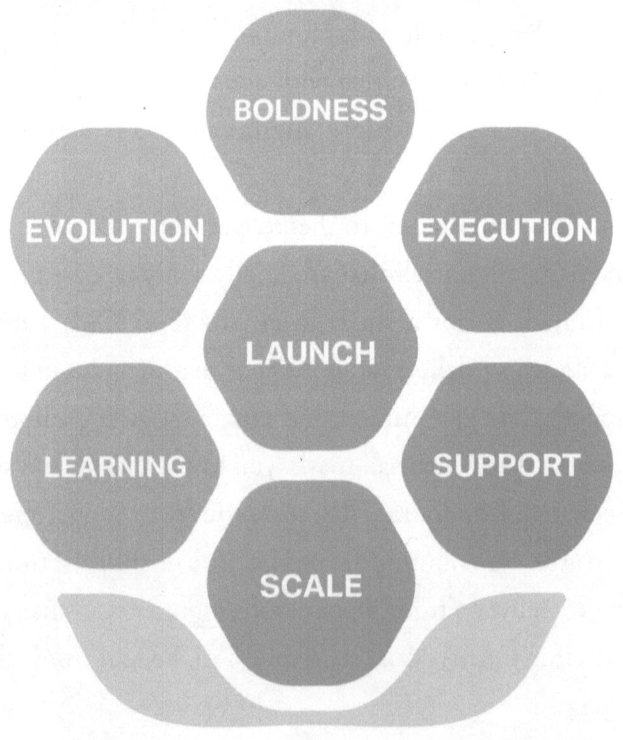

CHAPTER SIXTEEN

BOLDNESS

Nerve | Permission | Courage | Leap

Boldness is what gets you across the threshold from preparation into action. It's the courage to do the thing you've been building toward—to make your work public, to take up space, and to risk being seen and potentially criticized.

In Launch, boldness means moving forward despite fear, uncertainty, and the very real possibility of failure. It's trusting that you're ready enough, even when you don't feel completely ready.

Boldness is cultivated through action, not before it. You don't become bold and then launch. You launch, and the act of launching builds boldness.

The fears that show up at Launch are real, but they aren't always accurate. The brain treats visibility as threat—activating the same warning systems whether you're launching a new venture or facing physical danger. Understanding this helps you distinguish legitimate risk from mental resistance rooted in familiar stories.

Boldness in Launch is expressed through four dimensions: nerve, permission, courage, and leap.

NEUROSCIENCE NUGGET

Visibility activates the brain's threat-detection systems, triggering the same physiological responses used for physical danger. Taking action anyway rewires prediction circuits, teaching the brain that visibility is safe and building confidence through repetition.[14]

Nerve

Nerve is the raw capacity to do something that scares you. It's the willingness to feel fear and move forward anyway. Nerve isn't about eliminating nervousness; it's about acting despite it.

Nerve lives in the body first. Before your brain names the fear, your body registers it—elevated heart rate, butterflies in your stomach, tension across your chest. The mistake is waiting for these sensations to disappear before acting. Nerve means recognizing these as signals of significance—not danger—and moving forward while your body adjusts. With repetition, what once felt like alarm becomes familiar activation.

Everyone feels nervous before launching. The question isn't whether you'll feel it—it's whether you'll let it stop you. Nerve means recognizing that anxiety before a big moment is normal, expected, and doesn't mean you're not ready.

Nerve also comes from knowing you've done the work. You didn't skip steps. You designed thoughtfully, built carefully, and tested thoroughly. That preparation doesn't eliminate fear, but it gives you something solid to stand on when fear shows up.

---

14 Magness, *Do Hard Things*; Barrett, *Seven and a Half Lessons*.

Building nerve happens through exposure. Small acts of courage create confidence for bigger ones. Each time you do something that feels risky and you survive, your nervous system updates its threat assessment. What felt impossible becomes difficult, then manageable, then routine.

Permission

Permission is about authorizing yourself to take up space, share your work, and claim your expertise. External permission rarely comes. Launch requires giving yourself permission to begin.

Many accomplished people struggle with permission. They've built something valuable but feel they need more credentials, more experience, or more proof before they're "allowed" to launch. The wait for perfect conditions becomes its own form of resistance.

Permission work involves examining whose approval you're waiting for and why. Are you waiting for an authority figure to validate you? For perfect conditions that will never arrive? For certainty that doesn't exist? Often, what blocks Launch is lack of self-authorization, not lack of readiness.

Giving yourself permission doesn't mean ignoring feedback or claiming expertise you don't have. It means trusting that your current level of capability is enough to serve someone, somewhere, right now. You don't need to be the best—you need to be ready enough to help.

Courage

Courage is continuing to show up after the excitement fades, after setbacks occur, and after criticism arrives. Courage is what keeps you going when launching gets hard.

Courage doesn't mean you're not afraid. It means you've made peace with being afraid and you do the work anyway. You acknowledge the fear, assess whether it's pointing to real danger or just discomfort, and move forward with clear eyes.

Launch also includes the courage to be imperfect publicly. Your first launch won't be your best work. You'll make mistakes, miss things, and realize what you could have done better only after it's live. Courage means launching anyway, knowing you'll learn and improve as you go.

The most sustainable courage comes from connecting your launch to something bigger than yourself. When you're serving a purpose that matters deeply, when your work helps people who need what you're offering, courage becomes less about you and more about them. That shift changes everything.

Leap

This is "go time." Leap is the moment you actually do it. After all the preparation, all the planning, all the building—leap is when you hit publish, open the doors, send the email, or make the announcement.

The leap can be terrifying and liberating. Terrifying because once you launch, you can't take it back. Liberating because you're finally done preparing and starting to contribute. The leap transforms you from someone who's getting ready to someone who's doing the thing.

Readiness to leap often comes before the feeling of certainty. You've crossed from "not ready yet" to "ready enough now," even if it doesn't feel that way. The leap requires recognizing that moment and choosing to act.

The leap gets easier with practice. Your first launch will feel enormous. Your tenth will feel manageable. Each time you leap and survive—or better yet, succeed—you build evidence that leaping is survivable. That evidence accumulates and compounds.

Coaching Questions

- What is the action you've been avoiding that would create the biggest shift?
- If courage were the only requirement, what would you do next?
- What's the bold move your future self would make right now?

CHAPTER SEVENTEEN

EXECUTION

Presence | Activation | Pilot | Rollout

Execution is where the launch becomes real. It's the phase where your idea leaves the protected space of planning and steps into public contact. In the CCM, execution is not a single moment or a dramatic announcement; it is a structured sequence of intentional movement, visible presence, real-world testing, and sustained delivery. It is leadership in motion: clear choices, steady pacing, and consistent follow-through without burnout, panic, or frantic output. You've already clarified vision in Design and built capability in Build. Execution is where that work becomes visible, usable, and experienced by other people.

This phase requires both structure and self. Structure ensures you don't rely on adrenaline to push through. Self ensures you show up with presence, authenticity, and grounded authority. Together, they make your launch credible, sustainable, and real.

Execution unfolds across four expressions: presence, activation, pilot, and rollout.

NEUROSCIENCE NUGGET

Execution relies on shifting the brain from abstract planning networks into action-oriented learning systems. Repeated implementation strengthens neural pathways involved in habit formation and decision-making, turning effortful actions into efficient routines. The brain updates its expectations through real-world feedback—action is what rewires capability.[15]

Presence

Presence is the quality that gives your execution credibility. It's your ability to show up grounded, clear, and congruent—even in high-pressure moments when everything feels like it's riding on this one conversation, this one presentation, this one launch announcement.

Presence is the capacity to stand fully inside your message without shrinking back or overcompensating with false confidence. When you have genuine presence, people feel it immediately. They sense you believe what you're saying because you're not performing belief—you're embodying it.

Presence shows up in the subtle signals others read instinctively: your posture, your pacing, your breathing, your comfort with silence, your eye contact, your steadiness when challenged. It's your energy. It appears in how you handle unexpected questions, how you speak about your work without apologizing or overselling, and how you respond when things don't go according to plan. These moments are about authenticity.

Presence requires tools and practice—ways to ground yourself quickly, regulate your nervous system, and reconnect to your purpose rather than your performance anxiety.

---

15 Doidge, *The Brain That Changes Itself*; Rock, *Your Brain at Work*.

Presence also compounds over time. The more you practice showing up as yourself rather than as who you think you should be, the more natural it becomes. Your first launch might feel performative. Your fifth launch will feel like coming home to yourself. That's presence deepening through repetition and trust.

Activation

Activation is the moment when execution moves from presence to momentum. It's the shift from "I'm here" to "I'm in motion." In the CCM, activation is not intensity, pressure, or a dramatic push—it's deliberate sequencing. You turn intention into a living, breathing process. You meet the world not once but consistently.

Activation is strategic energy. You don't flood your system with urgency. You create rhythm. You choose what to release first, how to pace yourself, and how to communicate in a way that builds engagement rather than noise. Many launches fail not from lack of effort but from chaotic activation—too much, too fast, with no sustainable structure underneath. Activation solves that.

This is when plans, messaging, or early conversations begin. You're opening the door. Each action reinforces identity: You are someone who shows up, follows through, and takes responsibility for what you've built.

When you shift from thinking about your work to activating it, your nervous system receives evidence that this is real. Doubt loses power. Momentum becomes self-reinforcing. The hardest part is beginning—and activation ensures that beginning actually happens.

Pilot

Test in the Real World, Learn in Real Time

A pilot is where your work meets reality—carefully, intentionally, and in a way that offers learning without the pressure of perfection. In the CCM, a pilot is a smaller, strategic bridge between preparation and public rollout. It's designed to teach you what planning cannot.

A pilot could be a beta group, a soft opening, a trial run, or a limited-release offering. The purpose is clarity. What resonates? Where is the friction? What needs refinement? Real people interacting with your work will always reveal insights that testing cannot.

Piloting also strengthens confidence. Once your idea leaves the notebook and becomes something others can experience, you gain evidence—not assumptions—about its value. You learn how it feels to deliver it, what questions arise, what support structures you need, and what adjustments create greater ease and impact.

More importantly, a pilot accelerates momentum. It turns waiting into learning and learning into improvement. Every insight sharpens the full launch. Instead of building in isolation, you build with data, feedback, and lived experience.

Rollout

Expand your reach, build momentum, and stay visible.

Rollout begins after you've piloted, refined, and gained clarity. Your work is already alive in the world. Now, you're widening the circle. Rollout is the intentional amplification of something you've tested and believe in.

If pilot is a controlled test, rollout is a confident expansion.

Think of a rollout as widening the circle. You're scaling what already works. The emphasis is on cadence, visibility, and connection—showing up again and again in ways that feel sustainable.

Rollout is also adaptive. As more people encounter your work, you gather new signals: what resonates broadly, what needs simplifying, what sparks curiosity, and where people lean in. You adjust your message, strengthen your delivery, and expand your reach without abandoning your grounding.

The goal is momentum—steady, intentional, strategic momentum. Rollout ensures that what you've built has the impact you desire.

Coaching Questions

- Where does your work need to be seen next?
- What's the steady, sustainable rhythm that keeps you visible?
- What's one signal from your pilot that should shape your rollout?
- How will you maintain momentum without burning out?

CHAPTER EIGHTEEN

SUPPORT

Mentors | Allies | Systems | Accountability

Support is the stabilizing force of Launch. It's what keeps your work upright when the stakes rise, visibility increases, and pressure becomes real. During quiet Build seasons, it's possible to rely on willpower and improvisation. In Launch, those approaches break down. You need structures that hold you when energy fluctuates, when decisions accelerate, and when your nervous system is carrying more weight than usual.

Support keeps you present, grounded, and effective as momentum builds. Without support, launches become chaotic—fast starts followed by fast collapse. With support, launches become sustainable—a rhythm of contribution, recovery, iteration, and growth.

Strong support includes people, systems, boundaries, and accountability. It reduces decision fatigue, protects your energy, focuses your attention on what matters, and ensures you don't carry the emotional and logistical load alone. In Launch, you're not just managing a project—you're managing yourself. Support is how you stay well while leading.

Support in Launch unfolds across four dimensions: mentors, allies, systems, and accountability.

NEUROSCIENCE NUGGET

When you feel like you're carrying everything alone, you stay on high alert—triggering stress responses such as overthinking, avoidance, or shutdown. But when you bring in support—people who listen, collaborate, or simply believe in you—the nervous system shifts out of protection mode and into possibility. Support isn't weakness. It's a biological performance enhancer.

Social connection increases oxytocin, which lowers cortisol and calms the stress response, making hard tasks feel less overwhelming. It also activates neural pathways in the prefrontal cortex responsible for problem-solving, perspective, and motivation. Support doesn't just feel good; it changes how the brain operates.[16]

Mentors

Mentors are the people who've walked their own hard paths and are willing to share the truth of what they've learned. They don't tell you who to be; they remind you of who you already are by sharing their wisdom and direction. A mentor offers perspective you can't access from inside your own story. They help you see patterns, name fears, challenge assumptions, and trust your own voice.

During Launch, when vulnerability is high and things feel personal, a mentor provides steadiness. They normalize the discomfort

16 Lisa Feldman Barrett, *How Emotions Are Made: The Secret Life of the Brain* (Houghton Mifflin Harcourt, 2017); Magness, *Do Hard Things*.

that comes with being seen. They help you sort what's real from what's imagined. They hold up a mirror—not to judge you but to help you lead with clarity and courage.

Mentorship is about more than expertise. It's about generosity, honesty, and walking beside someone as they grow.

Allies

Allies are the people who stand with you, not above you. They're friends, peers, and partners who understand the courage it takes to build something new. Allies don't cheer from the sidelines. They sit with you in the middle, tell you the truth with compassion, and remind you that you're not alone.

In Launch, allies protect you from isolation. They help you stay grounded when your brain wants to spiral. They celebrate the small steps you'd overlook and call you forward when you want to shrink. They offer perspective, encouragement, and the kind of honest feedback that builds trust.

Allies create belonging and are with you along the journey, shoulder to shoulder.

Systems

Systems are what keep you steady when everything else speeds up. In Launch, they protect your energy, reduce decision fatigue, and create the structure that lets you show up present and clear—not rushed or reactive.

In Build, systems helped you learn. In Launch, they help you deliver. This is where routines, tools, and simple structures create a rhythm you can rely on: how you schedule, communicate, follow up, track interest, and stay visible even when your energy dips.

A good system makes success easier. It doesn't need to be complex. It might be a calendar that protects your best thinking time, a workflow that keeps opportunities from slipping through the cracks, or a weekly cadence that keeps your voice in the world. The goal is not sophistication—it's support.

The real purpose of systems is relief. When you're not holding everything in your head, you have the space to think clearly, listen deeply, and respond intentionally. Systems lighten the load so you can focus on what actually matters: the work, the people, and the impact you're building.

Accountability

Accountability is about staying connected to what you said matters. It's the structure that supports motivation wobbles or keeps you focused when life gets noisy.

During Launch, your energy can swing. Some days you feel unstoppable; other days you want to hide. That's normal. Accountability gives you a way to come back to center.

There are two kinds of accountability: *internal*, where you honor your word to yourself; and *external*, where someone you trust helps you stay aligned when doubt, distraction, or overwhelm kick in.

Healthy accountability isn't punitive. It's supportive. It's a check-in, not a callout. It helps you navigate the middle, adjust without shame, and recommit when you drift. It reminds you: You don't have to do this alone.

Accountability doesn't make the work easier.

It makes the work possible.

Coaching Questions

- Who is in your Launch support circle right now—and what role does each person actually play?
- Where are you relying on willpower when a system would serve you better?
- What kind of accountability helps you stay in motion without triggering pressure or shame?
- Where are you carrying something alone that was never meant to be carried solo?

CHAPTER NINETEEN

SCALE

Leverage | Efficiency | Sustainability | Growth

OK, you've launched successfully. Now how do you sustain and grow this launch without burning out?

That's what scale answers.

Scale isn't about doing more work or chasing endless expansion. It's about building an upward spiral—where what you've created can grow without requiring more of you at every turn. Scale is where your launch shifts from constantly creating to intelligently leveraging. From reinventing to refining. From effort-driven to structure-supported.

You've already done the hard work. You designed with clarity. You built capability and confidence. You launched with boldness. You executed with presence. You gathered support. Now, Scale asks: How do you make this sustainable? How do you grow without burning out?

The answer isn't hustle harder—it's build smarter.

Scale is about taking what's working and making it work harder for you. It's about turning onetime efforts into reusable systems. It's about processes becoming habitual so they run without constant mental load. It's about structured growth that builds on your foundation rather than starting from scratch every time.

When you scale well, your work compounds. Your time expands. Your impact grows. And you're not exhausted; you're energized because the structure is carrying weight you used to carry alone.

Scale unfolds through four pathways: leverage, efficiency, sustainability, and growth. Each one helps you build upward without burning out.

NEUROSCIENCE NUGGET

Scaling successfully depends on reducing cognitive load so the brain can focus on higher-value thinking instead of constant task switching. When systems automate routine decisions and lower mental effort, executive function is freed for creativity, strategy, and innovation. This shift strengthens the prefrontal cortex's capacity to plan, refine, and expand without triggering stress responses that lead to burnout.[17]

Leverage

Leverage is doing more with what you already have. It's the smartest move in scaling—letting your existing creation work harder for you instead of constantly creating new things from scratch.

Most people think growth requires new effort. New paths. New strategies. They exhaust themselves reinventing the wheel every time they want to expand. Leverage flips that entirely. It asks: What have you already built that could serve you in more ways, with less additional effort from you?

---

17 Rock, *Your Brain at Work*; Kahneman, *Thinking, Fast and Slow*.

In Launch, leverage shows up everywhere once you start looking for it. A live workshop you ran once becomes a recorded curriculum you can sell repeatedly. Client questions you answer individually become FAQ content that serves hundreds. A framework you use in coaching becomes a workbook, a course, or a keynote. You automate intake processes so onboarding doesn't require your direct involvement every time. You create templates that standardize delivery. You partner with people whose strengths amplify your reach without doubling your workload.

The key is recognizing that leverage isn't lazy—it's strategic. You're not cutting corners. You're building infrastructure that lets good work reach more people without requiring you to show up identically every single time.

Leverage also requires letting go of the belief that everything must be custom-built. Many high performers struggle here. They think personalization equals value, so they resist standardization. But here's the truth: Your core insight doesn't change whether you deliver it live to five people or provide it recorded to five hundred. The value is in the framework, not in reinventing it each time.

When leverage is working, you feel it immediately. Your time expands. Your work compounds. What used to take three hours now takes thirty minutes because you've built the system once and you're reusing it intelligently. Your launch operates more independently. You're not the single point of failure for everything.

Leverage also creates consistency, which builds trust. When you're not constantly scrambling to create from scratch, you refine what works. Your messaging sharpens. Your delivery improves. Your confidence grows because you're building on solid ground rather than starting over repeatedly.

The goal isn't to eliminate your presence—it's to multiply your impact without multiplying your effort. That's the power of leverage.

Efficiency

Efficiency is less about speed than it is about eliminating unnecessary friction. It's identifying what drains time and energy without creating corresponding value and then redesigning those processes so they work better.

Efficiency is often mistaken for doing more, faster. That's not what we're after. Real efficiency means doing the right things in the right order with the least wasted effort. It's about smooth flow, not frantic pace.

In Launch, efficiency shows up in your workflows. How many steps does it take for someone to sign up? How much back-and-forth happens in scheduling? How often are you manually doing something that could be automated? Each point of friction adds cognitive load and drains energy that could go toward higher-value work.

Start by mapping where friction lives. What feels harder than it should? What takes longer than necessary? What causes confusion or delay for you or your clients? These aren't just annoyances—they're opportunities for efficiency gains.

The solution isn't always technology. Sometimes efficiency means clearer communication that prevents confusion. Sometimes it's better sequencing that puts information where people need it when they need it. Sometimes it's eliminating a step entirely because it doesn't actually serve the outcome.

Efficiency also protects your energy for what matters most. When administrative tasks, communication, and delivery processes run smoothly, you have mental and emotional bandwidth for the work only you can do—strategy, creative thinking, meaningful connection with clients or customers.

The trap with efficiency is over-optimizing. You can spend so much time perfecting processes that you're no longer actually doing the work. Aim for "good enough to run smoothly" rather than "perfectly optimized." Efficiency serves your work—it doesn't become the work.

Sustainability

Sustainability is the factor that determines whether your launch becomes a career or just a sprint. Can you maintain this pace, this level of delivery, this commitment—not for three months but for three years?

Many launches don't fail because they didn't work initially but because they weren't designed to last. People burn out. Systems break down. The initial excitement fades, and what remains doesn't feel sustainable. Sustainability asks you to design for the long game from the beginning.

Sustainability requires honest assessment of your capacity. What can you actually maintain without depleting yourself? What rhythms support your energy rather than drain it? What boundaries protect your ability to show up consistently over time?

This means building recovery into your rhythm, not treating it as something you'll get to later. It means pricing your work to support your life, not just cover expenses. It means saying no to opportunities that would compromise your ability to deliver well on existing commitments.

Sustainability also means designing your business model or project structure to support longevity. Recurring revenue is more sustainable than constantly chasing onetime sales. Leveraged delivery is more sustainable than trading time for money at every turn. Systems that run without your constant intervention are more sustainable than being the single point of contact for everything.

The deeper work of sustainability is internal. It's managing your relationship with ambition so growth doesn't come at the cost of health. It's recognizing when you're operating from scarcity or fear rather than strategic intention. It's building a life around your work that actually supports the work rather than competing with it.

Sustainable launches don't just survive—they thrive because they're designed to last. They create consistent value without consuming the person delivering it. That's the goal.

Growth

Growth is the natural result when leverage, efficiency, and sustainability are working together. It's not forced expansion; it's organic development that emerges from solid infrastructure.

Smart growth isn't about doing more of everything. It's about identifying what's working and intentionally expanding that while letting go of what isn't serving your vision. Growth requires discernment—knowing what to scale and what to release.

In Launch, growth happens in stages. First, you stabilize—making sure what you've launched actually works and can be delivered consistently. Then, you refine—improving based on feedback and learning what resonates most. Only after stabilization and refinement do you amplify—reaching more people, expanding offerings, or increasing capacity.

Growth works if you stabilize first. Expanding too soon creates chaos, not momentum. People add new offerings before the first one is running smoothly. They expand their audience before they've proven they can serve the current one well. This creates chaos rather than growth. Real growth builds on a stable foundation.

Growth also requires letting go. As you scale, some things that worked at launch won't work at the next level. Some clients who were perfect early on won't be the right fit as you evolve. Some processes that served you initially will need to be retired. Growth means releasing what got you *here* to make room for what gets you *there*.

The most sustainable growth is intentional and aligned. You're not growing because you think you should or because comparison tells you to; you're growing because it serves your mission, supports your vision, and feels like natural evolution rather than forced expansion.

When growth is working, it feels like momentum rather than pressure. You're building on what's solid, expanding what's proven, and evolving in ways that energize rather than exhaust you.

Coaching Questions

- What's working that you can do more of with less effort?
- What structure or system would make this sustainable—not exhausting?
- Where can processes replace willpower so you don't have to carry everything?

CHAPTER TWENTY

LEARNING

Reflection | Data | Discernment | Synthesis

Launch generates information. Learning is what you do with that information.

In the CCM, learning is both observation and action. You're not just collecting feedback or tracking metrics; you're interpreting what the data means, discerning what matters from what's noise, and integrating insights so they actually change how you operate.

Learning transforms Launch from a onetime event into an evolution. Each conversation, each pilot, each piece of feedback becomes intelligence that sharpens your approach. The first version of anything is rarely the best version. Learning is how you close that gap.

The challenge is that Launch creates overwhelm. Information floods in faster than you can process it. Some feedback contradicts other feedback. Metrics tell different stories depending on how you read them. Without deliberate learning practices, valuable insights get lost in the chaos.

Learning requires creating space—actual time and mental bandwidth—to step back from doing and reflect on what's working, what's not, and why. It means valuing the pause that feels unproductive but actually makes everything else more effective.

Learning unfolds through four practices: reflection, data, discernment, and synthesis.

NEUROSCIENCE NUGGET

Learning requires mental distance because insight emerges when the brain shifts out of task-focused mode into a more reflective state. This activates the brain's default mode network, enabling pattern recognition, perspective-taking, and meaning-making. When people pause to reflect rather than stay in constant execution, the brain integrates experience into new neural pathways—turning action into growth instead of repetition.[18]

Reflection

Reflection is the intentional pause that turns experience into insight. It's stepping back from the intensity of Launch to ask: What's actually happening here? What are you learning? What wants to shift?

Without reflection, you repeat the same patterns without recognizing them. You stay reactive instead of strategic. You miss the lessons hiding in plain sight because you're moving too fast to notice them.

Reflection doesn't require elaborate processes. It can be ten minutes at the end of each week asking yourself what worked, what didn't work, and what you'd do differently. It can be debriefing a difficult conversa-

---

18 Boyatzis et al., *Helping People Change.*

tion to understand what triggered your response. It can be journaling about what energized or drained you during Launch.

The power of reflection lies in creating distance. When you're inside an experience, you can't see it clearly. Reflection gives you perspective—the ability to observe your own patterns, recognize what's driving your choices, and identify where adjustments would serve you.

Reflection also builds self-awareness, which is the foundation of all growth. When you understand why you react the way you do, why certain feedback lands harder than other feedback, and why some aspects of Launch feel natural while others feel forced, you can make better decisions about what to keep, change, or release.

The trap with reflection is overthinking. You can analyze yourself into paralysis. The goal isn't perfect understanding—it's useful insight that informs better action.

Data

Data is the objective evidence of what's working and what's not. It's the metrics, feedback, and observable results that tell you whether your launch is creating the impact you intended.

The challenge with data is knowing what to measure. You could track everything—website visits, email open rates, conversion percentages, engagement metrics, revenue, customer satisfaction, referral sources, steps taken per day, minutes spent meditating, hours spent at the gym. But not all data matters equally. The key is identifying leading indicators that predict success and lagging indicators that confirm results.

Data also requires honest interpretation. It's easy to cherry-pick numbers that support what you want to believe while ignoring data that challenges your assumptions. Real learning happens when you're willing to see what the data actually shows, not just what you hoped it would show.

Some of the most valuable data isn't quantitative—it's qualitative. What are people actually saying? What questions keep coming up? What misunderstandings persist? What language resonates? This kind of data reveals gaps between your intention and their experience.

Data becomes useful when it informs decisions. If you're tracking metrics but not adjusting based on what you learn, you're collecting information without extracting value. The point isn't perfect measurement—it's actionable insight.

Discernment

Discernment is knowing what matters. It's the ability to separate signal from noise, wisdom from opinion, useful feedback from projection.

Launch generates overwhelming input. Everyone has an opinion. Some feedback is gold. Some is garbage. Some reflects real problems. Some reflects individual preferences that don't represent your broader audience. Discernment is how you navigate this without either dismissing everything or letting everything derail you.

Discernment requires clarity about your vision and values. When you know what you're building and whom you're serving, you can evaluate feedback against that standard. Does this input help you serve your audience better? Does it align with your values? Does it move you toward your vision or pull you away from it?

Not all feedback deserves equal weight. Feedback from people who've actually engaged with your work matters more than opinions from people observing from the sidelines. Feedback that shows up repeatedly across different sources matters more than one person's strong reaction. Feedback that points to genuine confusion or misalignment matters more than subjective preferences.

Discernment also means recognizing when criticism is about you versus about your work. Attacks on your credibility, character, or worthiness aren't useful feedback—they're someone else's issues showing up as noise. Learning to filter these attacks out protects your energy and keeps you focused on meaningful improvement.

The practice of discernment gets easier over time. You develop a sense for what rings true versus what feels off. You learn to trust your gut while staying open to challenge. You get better at holding feedback lightly enough to consider it without letting it destabilize you.

Synthesis

Synthesis is where learning becomes usable. It's the moment when you take everything you've gathered—reflection, data, and discernment—and ask: So, what does all of this mean?

Without synthesis, insights stay scattered. You have observations without conclusions and patterns without meaning. Synthesis is the work of combining what you've learned into clarity you can act on.

Synthesis asks: Given what you've reflected on, what the data shows, and what you've discerned actually matters—what's the insight? What's the pattern? What's the takeaway?

Synthesis often happens in conversation—with a coach, mentor, or thought partner who can help you connect dots you can't see alone. It happens in writing, when you articulate what you're learning. It happens in quiet moments, when your brain finally has the space to make meaning from the noise.

The goal is some sense of clarity—of weaving what you've learned into your vision, dreams, goals, and next actions.

Coaching Questions

- Given everything you've learned, what's the core insight?
- What pattern is emerging that you need to pay attention to?
- What does this mean for how you move forward?

CHAPTER TWENTY-ONE

EVOLUTION

Rest | Renewal | Resilience | Transformation

You launched. You learned. You integrated.

Now the question becomes: What's next?

Evolution is the moment when you stop treating success as a finish line and start treating it as a foundation. It's when the chapter you built becomes the chapter you grow.

Evolution isn't reinvention for its own sake. It's not burning everything down because you got bored or endlessly chasing the next shiny idea. It's about taking what works and making it work even better. It's about letting your experience inform smarter choices. It's about refining instead of repeating.

You evolve on purpose, not by accident.

Here's the truth:

Version 1.0 got you here.

But versions 2.0, 3.0, 4.0—that's where the real impact happens.

Evolution asks:

What's becoming possible now that wasn't possible before?

What did you learn that changes how you operate?

What deserves expansion?

What needs to level up?

Sometimes evolution is a small adjustment.

Sometimes it's a major shift.

Sometimes it's a complete redefinition of what you're building—or who you're becoming.

And here's the beautiful part: Evolution compounds. Every insight, every improvement, and every upgrade stacks. Over time, you don't just maintain momentum—you multiply it.

Evolution unfolds through four pathways: rest, renewal, resilience, and transformation.

Together, they turn a successful launch into a living system—one that grows, adapts, and keeps getting better.

Because greatness isn't built from a single breakthrough. It's built from continuous becoming.

NEUROSCIENCE NUGGET

The brain doesn't change in a single leap—it changes through repetition. Every time you apply a new insight, run a new behavior, or interrupt an old pattern, your brain reinforces the neural pathways that support that change. Over time, tiny adjustments become automatic responses. That's neuroplasticity in action: evolution through iteration.

Research shows that sustainable transformation comes from updating your internal models again and again—not from one breakthrough moment. Small corrections compound. Each cycle of trying, evaluating, and adjusting physically reshapes the brain, making new behaviors more natural and old habits less dominant.[19]

Rest

Rest isn't weakness. It's strategy.

Your brain, body, and nervous system cannot operate at Launch intensity indefinitely. Rest is how you restore the cognitive capacity, emotional regulation, and physical energy required to sustain performance. Without it, everything degrades—decision-making, creativity, emotional stability, and physical health.

The challenge is that some highly motivated achievers treat rest as something earned after proving productivity. This is backwards. Rest enables productivity. When you skip recovery, you don't maintain capacity—you erode it. What feels like pushing through is actually depleting the resources you need for sustained excellence.

Rest happens at multiple timescales: between tasks (stepping away from your screen, taking a breath, and shifting your attention), daily (sleep and genuine downtime), weekly (dedicated rest days), and seasonally (breaks between major projects or launches).

Effective rest requires actually disengaging. Checking email during "rest time" isn't recovery. Worrying about work during vacation isn't recovery. Rest means giving your brain, body, and nervous system permission to stop monitoring, managing, and problem-solving.

Rest also requires redefining productivity. Your worth isn't measured by constant output. Some of your most valuable work happens when you're not working—when your brain consolidates learning, generates insights, and restores the capacity for focused attention.

19 Costandi, *Neuroplasticity*; Adam Grant, *Think Again: The Power of Knowing What You Don't Know* (Viking, 2021).

Renewal

Renewal is rest with intention. It's not just stopping; it's actively replenishing what Launch depleted.

Launch drains specific resources: creative energy, emotional capacity, mental clarity, physical stamina, and social connection. Renewal means identifying what got depleted and intentionally restoring it. If Launch drained your creative reserves, renewal might mean engaging with art, music, or nature. If it drained emotional capacity, renewal might mean time with people who fill you up rather than people who need things from you.

Renewal also reconnects you to what matters beyond the work. Launch can consume your identity—you become "the person doing this thing" rather than a whole human with multiple dimensions. Renewal reminds you that you exist beyond your accomplishments. You have relationships, interests, values, and experiences that have nothing to do with your professional impact.

The practice of renewal requires knowing yourself. What actually restores you? What activities, environments, or connections fill your tank rather than drain it? For some people, renewal is solitude. For others, it's community. For some, it's physical movement. For others, it's creative expression. There's no formula—only what works for you.

Renewal isn't indulgence. It's maintenance. You can't pour from an empty cup, and Launch empties cups fast. Renewal ensures you have something to give when the next challenge, opportunity, or phase begins.

Resilience

Resilience is your capacity to navigate setbacks without breaking. It's not about avoiding challenges; it's about developing the internal resources to meet them without collapsing.

Launch will test you. Things won't go as planned. Feedback will sting. Technology will fail. People will disappoint you. Your own doubts will surface. Resilience is what keeps you moving forward when everything feels hard.

Resilience isn't something you either have or don't have; it's something you build. It develops through facing challenges, learning you can survive them, and integrating that evidence into your sense of capability. Each time you navigate difficulty and come out the other side, you strengthen the neural pathways that support resilience.

Resilience also comes from perspective. When you remember that this moment isn't forever, that setbacks are information rather than verdicts, and that challenge is part of growth rather than evidence of failure, you can stay grounded when things get hard. Resilience means holding both the difficulty and the bigger picture simultaneously.

The foundation of resilience is self-trust. When you know you've handled hard things before, when you trust your ability to figure things out, and when you believe in your capacity to adapt, challenges become less threatening. You're not unaffected by difficulty, but you're not destroyed by it either.

Resilience requires support. No one successfully navigates hard things alone. The people who stay resilient have relationships, practices, and structures that help them process difficulty, maintain perspective, and access encouragement when their own reserves run low.

Transformation

Transformation is the recognition that you're not the same person who started this journey. Launch changes you. The question isn't whether you'll transform—it's whether you'll let the transformation be conscious and intentional.

You've faced fears, developed capabilities, navigated complexity, and stepped into visibility. You've learned things about yourself—your strengths, your edges, your patterns, your capacity. You've discovered what matters most when stakes are high. That changes you at a fundamental level.

Transformation asks you to integrate who you're becoming with who you've been. You're not abandoning your former self—you're expanding. The version of you that started Design had certain assumptions, limitations, and possibilities. The version of you completing Launch operates from different ground. Acknowledge that growth.

Transformation also requires releasing what no longer serves you—old identities, outdated beliefs, relationships that constrain rather than support, patterns that worked before but don't work now. Growth means letting go of what got you *here* to make room for what gets you *there*.

The deepest transformation isn't about what you accomplished; it's about who you became in the process. You didn't just launch something. You became someone capable of launching. That shift in identity is more valuable than any single achievement because it's transferable to everything that comes next.

Transformation is both an ending and a beginning. This chapter closes. The next one opens. And you enter it different from the way you were before—more capable, more clear, more confident in your ability to design, build, and launch your next big thing.

Coaching Questions

- What deserves to grow, improve, or expand now that the big chapter has launched?
- What becomes possible in version 2.0 of you that wasn't possible in version 1.0?

- What is your next big chapter?

____

____

____

____

____

____

____

____

____

____

Integration Bridge: The Continuous Cycle

FROM LAUNCH BACK TO DESIGN—AGAIN AND AGAIN

You've moved through the complete cycle. You designed with clarity. You built with intention. You launched with courage. You learned. You evolved.

And now? You do it again.

The CCM isn't a onetime journey. It's a continuous practice—a framework you'll return to again and again, at every scale, for every next big thing you create.

THE CYCLE EXPANDS WITH YOU

Design-Build-Launch works at every timescale. You might move through the complete cycle daily—designing your morning, building focus, launching into action, learning from what worked, and evolving your approach for tomorrow. You might work the cycle weekly—

designing your priorities, building systems, launching initiatives, reflecting on progress, and renewing for the next week.

You might navigate the cycle monthly or quarterly—designing projects, building capability, launching offerings, integrating feedback, and transforming your approach. Or you might move through it annually—designing your next chapter, building infrastructure, launching publicly, scaling impact, and evolving your identity.

The framework serves you at whatever scale your growth requires. Some cycles take hours. Some take years. What matters isn't the duration—it's the practice of moving through Design-Build-Launch with intention, learning, and evolution.

THE SPIRAL UPWARD

Each time you complete the cycle, you're not starting over. You're spiraling upward. The insights from this launch inform your next design. The capabilities you built become the foundation for what you build next. The confidence you developed through launching makes the next launch feel less terrifying. The resilience you cultivated prepares you for bigger challenges ahead.

You're not the same person beginning the next cycle. You bring with you everything you learned, everything you became, and everything you now know you're capable of. Each pass through Design-Build-Launch compounds. You get faster. You get wiser. You get braver.

WHEN TO REENTER

The beauty of this framework is its flexibility. You don't always need to start at Design and move linearly through to evolution. You reenter wherever you need support.

Feeling unclear or stuck? Return to Design. Refine your vision. Clarify your scope. Redesign your approach based on what you've learned.

Need to develop capability or test ideas? Move into Build. Strengthen your tools. Prototype new approaches. Build confidence through deliberate practice.

Ready to contribute publicly? Enter Launch. Execute with presence. Scale what's working. Learn from real-world feedback.

The framework isn't rigid; it's responsive. It meets you where you are and guides you toward where you're going.

THE PRACTICE OF CONTINUOUS EVOLUTION

What you've learned isn't just a methodology for this project. It's how you'll navigate transformation for the rest of your life.

Every time you face a new challenge, pursue a new vision, or step into a new chapter, you'll return to this framework. Design the clarity. Build the capability. Launch with courage. Learn from the experience. Evolve through the process.

This is how growth becomes sustainable. This is how ambition becomes achievable. This is how transformation becomes a practice rather than a crisis.

You now have a complete system for designing, building, and launching your next big thing—and the one after that, and the one after that.

THE NEXT DESIGN AWAITS

So, ask yourself: What wants to be designed next?

What new vision is calling you forward? What capability wants to be built? What contribution wants to be launched? What learning wants to be integrated? What transformation wants to emerge?

The cycle continues. The spiral rises. The work evolves.

And you? You're ready.

Welcome back to Design.

PRACTICE

THE METHOD IN ACTION

CHAPTER TWENTY-TWO

MY COACHING PALETTE

One of the most common questions I'm asked by prospective clients, colleagues, or curious peers is some version of: "What kind of coach are you?" It's a fair question. In an industry that's growing rapidly and filled with countless approaches, niches, and philosophies, people want clarity. They want to understand not just what I do but how I do it and, more importantly, who I do it for.

My coaching works in the present-to-future space—less about processing the past, more about designing what's next.

Figure 5: Five Modes of Development

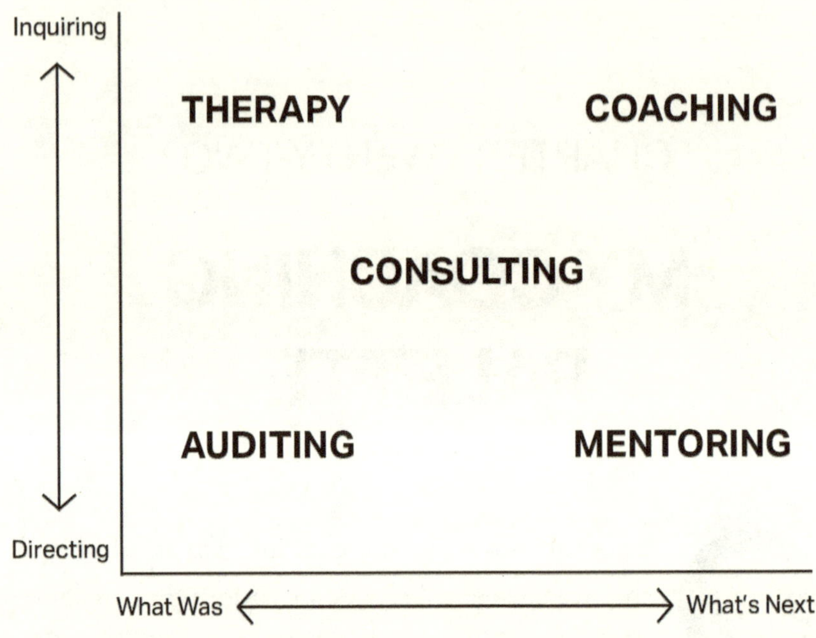

These five modes of development—coaching, mentoring, consulting, auditing, and therapy—are often confused or collapsed into one another. In practice, they differ based on two primary dimensions: whether the work is more inquiring or directing, and whether it orients toward what was or what's next. Therapy and auditing focus on understanding and diagnosing the past through different lenses. Coaching and mentoring are more present and future-facing, supporting growth through inquiry and experience. Consulting sits at the center, translating insight into solutions and action. While each mode has a distinct center of gravity, coaching, mentoring, and consulting sometimes overlap and flow together—with coaching leading the way.

Within this future-facing space, I focus on coaching the whole person.

I know there are some coaching approaches that aim to simply optimize the client's performance in a narrow lane by applying a rigid, step-by-step framework to every challenge. With the CCM, however, the goal is more holistic in nature and seeks to create opportunities for growth in all aspects of the client's life experience.

I've seen firsthand that real progress—the kind that earns truly transformative results, not just a temporary alteration in behavior—doesn't necessarily come from a myopic focus on a singular issue.

Instead, I find with the majority of my clients that the more fulfilling results are achieved when we work together to address the full spectrum of who someone really is: their goals, of course, but also their fears, their story, their values, their blind spots, and their vision of what's possible.

So, while some coaching systems offer their clients cookie-cutter formulas and one-size-fits-all solutions, I prefer a much more personal and custom-tailored approach. Every client I work with is navigating their journey with their own context, obstacles, and definition of success. My role isn't to force them to conform that journey to my framework but rather to open them to their fullest potential.

In that regard, when I'm working with my clients, I'm not following a hard script or expecting the same results from clients who are absolutely unique in their makeup and ambitions. Instead, I see my role as an experienced guide to walk beside them as they explore a trail for the first time—listening intently not only to what they say but also to the subtle, unspoken clues of which they are often unaware. Sometimes, I take the lead with a story or by applying a tool, with a tailored approach that honors the complexity of real life. Sometimes, I challenge them and their preconceived notions—especially their limiting beliefs. Always, I am there to champion their cause (more about that in a moment).

Over time, I've built a broad, dynamic, and deeply integrated coaching toolbox. It's not a static set of tricks but a living, evolving palette of methodologies, perspectives, and disciplines that I draw from based on what's needed in the moment. Some days, we're navigating the corporate strategies in a workplace where they're looking to advance. Other days, we're untangling self-doubt or the other self-sabotaging behaviors that trip them up before they start. And often, it's a combination of these and still more considerations.

That's the nature of human-centered growth. Because it simply doesn't happen in silos; it happens in real time to real people.

Here's a look at the core coaching modalities and dimensions I work with. Remember, these are not separate compartments but rather interwoven threads in the tapestry of transformation.

Executive Leadership Coaching: A Clearer View from the Summit

Success doesn't make things easier. The higher you climb, the more complexity you carry—ambiguity, expectations, politics, shifting markets, diverse teams, and the weight of being the one everyone looks to for answers.

When you're the one everyone turns to, where do you turn?

You need a neutral, impartial partner—someone outside the org chart with no agenda except your growth.

I've spent decades in numerous Fortune 100 companies. I've been in the proverbial trenches, from individual contributor to leading global teams. I understand the role because I've lived it.

I work with executives, entrepreneurs, and emerging leaders who need a strategic partner to cut through noise and think out loud. I say what their superiors won't and their subordinates can't. I challenge assumptions, pressure-test decisions, enable presence, and help them move forward with clarity.

Leadership today demands more than authority—it requires presence and authenticity.

I work with many who are stepping into larger, more ambitious roles or working to find more fulfillment while staying in place.

High stakes. Higher potential.

Neuroscience-Based Coaching: The Science of Change and Growth

I've met many smart, analytical people who don't just want coaching protocols—they want to know why coaching works. I'm the same way.

We all know people who've tried their best, followed programs, set intentions—and still slid back into old behaviors. Maybe that's been you.

Here's one reason why: Your brain has been wiring itself for decades, reinforcing patterns through repetition. Some serve you. Others hold you back. Any effort to change is a direct challenge to your brain's preference for the status quo.

But here's what matters: Your brain never stops changing. This is neuroplasticity.

We can interrupt old patterns and create space for new ones. When you shift perspective, challenge assumptions, or connect insight to emotion, you're not just thinking differently—you're building new neural pathways.

Embodiment is central to this work. Your body constantly informs your thoughts, emotions, and decisions. Awareness means learning to read those signals—what does alignment feel like? Where does resistance show up? Creation happens when you act on that awareness, prototyping new behaviors. Growth emerges as repetition makes new patterns feel natural.

That's why you'll find Neuroscience Nuggets throughout the Design-Build-Launch framework. They're the science behind why coaching works.

Personal (Life) Coaching: Integration and Alignment

In the course of my practice, I find this to be the most human dimension of coaching and, in many ways, the most foundational. No matter how ambitious your career goals or how complex your leadership challenges, everything is built on the same ground: you.

If you'll think about it for a moment, "you" is a much more complicated concept than you might first consider. It's far more than just you as a person. It's your well-being and your relationships. It's your sense of purpose and your ability to live a life that feels not just productive but meaningful. Every part of your life makes up *you*.

Because of this, personal coaching is about developing awareness and creativity and then integrating them. It's the work of aligning the external and internal versions of all of the many elements of you: who you are, what you value, and how you show up in the world.

So, in my capacity as a personal coach, I work with my clients to look at their habits, priorities, boundaries, and relationships as well as the unspoken patterns that have been shaping their choices.

But this is about far more than just optimizing every corner of your calendar or hacking your way into productivity. It's about an even more significant alignment.

And that process begins with one simple question: What does fulfillment look like for you, really? And what needs to shift to make space for that?

Once we've identified that destination, we can begin to set the course necessary to make the journey to personal self-realization and self-satisfaction.

Because at the end of the day, it's not just about achieving more; that's no longer enough. Instead, it's all about becoming a more fully realized version of you.

Career Coaching: Expanding Scope and Impact

Perhaps you've reached that moment when looking back on your career causes you to look forward and ask: What's next?

Many of my clients are ambitious, constantly taking on new challenges and always striving for that next progression on their career path. Some of them are considering a lateral move or making an even bolder leap into a completely new industry. There are more than a few who are contemplating a complete reinvention—something I know more than a little about, personally.

Because I'm intimately aware of the many aspects of making this kind of change in one's life, I know all too well that this transition is about more than résumés and LinkedIn updates. It's about fully developing one's professional identity with a fully realized vision and consciously designing the life you want to live.

To accomplish this, a client needs someone who's been on both sides of the hiring table, like I have—both as a candidate hopeful for a promising position and as an executive whose sole focus is on building the most powerful team possible. I'm someone who's submitted dozens of résumés over the years and someone who's seen thousands of résumés, interviewed hundreds of people, and hired many applicants over my corporate career. When those in hiring positions tell a candidate that they're looking for the person with the right fit, I know exactly what that quality looks like to your next employer. And if you're looking for a coach to assist you in achieving those sorts of professional ambitions, you need a coach who understands what real career transformation requires.

Together, my clients and I clarify where they're going and why. We examine their professional journey and identify the themes, strengths, and aspirations ready to be activated. Then, we build a strategy—not only for getting the next job but also for designing the next chapter.

Because my goal isn't simply to hand my client a script, I am uniquely positioned to empower my clients to become the author of their next professional phase with intention, clarity, and confidence.

Mentorship: Experience That Accelerates Growth

Mentorship is where my personal experience becomes leverage for my clients' aspirational journeys. Though I bring more traditional modalities such as models and frameworks to my coaching work when they serve a purpose and are appropriate, I find that effective mentorship is more about lived experience and lessons earned in the trenches. And, in that way, I can offer the kind of perspective that's only available from one such as myself, who has personally led global teams, made those hard executive decisions, and successfully navigated identity shifts through major transitions.

By referencing the arc of my own leadership journey, I'm uniquely positioned to offer informed insights that drastically accelerate my clients' progress and development. That might mean unpacking how I navigated complex dynamics, handled high-stakes pivots, or found my footing again after a major transition. It may mean letting my clients know that I understand all too well just how difficult this terrain can be and how it can take a serious toll on all aspects of one's life experience if not handled effectively.

Mentorship is a distinct form of coaching. It's less open-ended exploration, more guided growth. But I cherish the moments when I'm able to share with my clients, "I've been there. Here's what I learned. Here's how you might think about it."

Done my way, mentoring helps my clients sidestep pitfalls, lead with clarity, and move forward with the confidence of someone who knows they're not on this journey alone.

Thought Partnership: Thinking Better Together

Sometimes, the most powerful coaching comes not through serving my clients but through working with them and thinking together. As I practice it, the essence of thought partnership is a relationship in which the client's ideas are stretched, challenged, and sharpened through collaborative dialogue.

My clients come to me not necessarily because they're stuck but because they're on the edge of something big. They're navigating complexity, evaluating trade-offs, or standing at the crossroads of multiple good options. And what they need in those high-stakes scenarios isn't a map but a mirror—a thinking partner who can ask questions, surface blind spots, and help you see the landscape more clearly.

Thought partnership is potent for entrepreneurs, executives, creatives, visionaries, and all those whose work lives at the intersection of innovation and uncertainty. And it almost always leads to breakthroughs that wouldn't have happened alone.

Entrepreneur Coaching: Building Something That Lasts

Starting something from scratch isn't for the faint of heart. Whether it's a company, consultancy, creative venture, or personal brand, ground-up development demands more than just a good idea. It calls for resilience in uncertainty, maintaining vision under pressure, and belief in a mission bigger than yourself.

Riding the roller coaster of entrepreneurship—one day riding the high of possibility and then, the next, questioning everything—is not for the weak in spirit. And those who want to take on that challenge need a reliable presence to steady them through that volatility—someone who offers perspective, strategy, and support.

Whether a client is refining their offer, building their business model, or scaling their leadership, they need help staying grounded in the big picture without losing their grip on the day-to-day. Think of it as a North Star to steer by when the seas get rough.

Because, when it all comes down to it, entrepreneurship is more than a job—it's a life mission. And I'm here to help my clients build something that reflects their brilliance and values and that rewards their personal investment and hard work.

Consultative Coaching: Strategy Meets Support

Sometimes, a client faces complex challenges that require both strategic thinking and personal clarity. That is, they need someone who is comfortable leaving the usual space of the coach and who can actively help them clarify goals, identify root causes, and map the terrain.

While this functionality comprises a relatively small part of my coaching palette, there are times that I offer my clients the same rigor to coaching that I brought to managing large teams and scaling global systems in the tech world: clarity, analysis, and an unflinching focus on outcomes.

And while this draws on my corporate experience, the approach remains deeply human—because even the most complex problems are solved by people.

This hybrid approach—part coach, part corporate strategist—gives my clients both the tools needed to assess their situations and the confidence required to move forward decisively.

CHAPTER TWENTY-THREE

CLIENT SCENARIOS

Coaching Real People, Real Transformations

Frameworks are powerful, but they don't change lives until they meet real people, real pressures, and real decisions. The CCM is built to work in the real world—inside demanding jobs, busy families, financial realities, and uncertain futures. These scenarios show what happens when Design-Build-Launch stops being a concept and becomes a practice. You'll see how clarity creates momentum, how small prototypes reshape careers, and how intentional systems help people evolve without burning out or blowing up their lives.

Each client entered coaching from a different starting point—some at a peak, some stuck, some burned out, some simply ready for more—but every one of them was asking the same question: *What's next?* Through Design, they found clarity. Through Build, they created momentum. Through Launch, they shaped new identities and new realities. These are not stories of overnight transformation. They are stories of iteration, alignment, courage, and follow-through. And they show that when you design your life with intention, the next chapter isn't discovered—it's built.

What follows are five true-to-life scenarios that illustrate how Design-Build-Launch works across different careers, life stages, identities, and ambitions.

Client Scenario 1

MAX: FROM THE CURRENT SUMMIT TO CREATING THE NEXT ASCENT

Max is a seasoned tech executive known for scaling high-growth teams and launching big global initiatives. He's climbed steadily and built deep expertise while leading teams in big tech, having earned every stripe and his seat at the table. He's worked with coaches before. In fact, nearly every senior level executive he knows has a coach in their corner. It's what great companies do—pay for coaching because they know that working with an impartial, strategic partner produces return on investment many times over.

Max has found himself standing on the summit he once dreamed of. The big job? Nailed it. Impact? Proven. Compensation? Done very well. But this was never the finish line.

Lately, something's shifted. The pace still excites him, but the structure feels tight. He's felt this before and talks openly with his boss and mentors about the next move. He's not ready to retire, but he wants more than the next promotion. He wants to remain challenged while reclaiming freedom, re-innovate his identity, and expand his impact—without blowing everything up. Also, his kids are teenagers now, and he's realizing how much he's missing.

And there's something else: Max is starting to think beyond this next chapter. What comes after the next summit? Semiretirement?

Entrepreneurship? Board work? Full retirement? He doesn't have answers yet, but he knows his next move needs to position him well for whatever follows.

That's what brought him to coaching—not a crisis but strategic questions: What does the freedom to create my next chapter actually look like? How do I expand my impact without starting over? How do I design this next move so it sets me up for the chapter after that?

THE CCM IN ACTION

Max worked through the Design-Build-Launch framework over twelve months, moving through multiple iterations. The method is agile—we started with clarity work in Design but quickly moved into Build and Launch to generate momentum and test ideas. Each phase informed the others. Action created clarity. Data refined direction.

THE START: HEAVY DESIGN, EARLY BUILD

We began with foundational clarity. Max completed the Cloudberry values assessment, identifying what mattered most to him now. Eight values rose to the top, creating productive tension:

- Strategic impact: His work needed to matter at scale.
- Innovation: He craved the edge of what's next, not maintaining what already worked.
- Autonomy: He wanted control over how he worked, not just what he worked on.
- Collaboration: Small, high-trust teams energized him more than hierarchy.
- Growth: He needed intellectual challenge, not comfort.

- Flexibility: Every choice needed to expand future possibilities, not narrow them.
- Family: His kids were teenagers, and he wanted to be present.
- Service: He wanted to use his expertise to contribute to his community and help others grow.

These values became his decision filter. Any opportunity had to honor most of them, or it wasn't worth pursuing. Saying no to options, at times, is more important than what we say yes to.

Max noticed something interesting: Just thinking about AI work energized him in a way his current role didn't, even though the AI work would be objectively harder. When work aligns with values, the brain releases neurochemicals that increase focus and motivation. His brain was rewarding the alignment.

From values, vision emerged. Max painted two horizons. The immediate summit was leading a high-stakes initiative in emerging technology with small-team dynamics and meaningful autonomy. The longer view was positioning himself for board work, advisory roles, or entrepreneurship in five to seven years.

Ambitions became more specific. Take on work that reignites intellectual engagement. Build deep expertise in AI and emerging tech. Create a work model that doesn't require sixty-hour weeks. Develop a reputation as a strategic thought leader *and* a global product launch expert. These ambitions informed more specific goals that were actionable, measurable, and trackable.

Identity work surfaced next. Who was Max becoming? He named it: a strategic leader building toward long-term freedom. This wasn't about stepping back; it was about stepping up differently.

While this clarity work continued, Max started prototyping immediately. He volunteered to lead a cross-functional AI exploration initiative while still in his current role—testing whether emerging tech leadership excited him as much as he hoped.

He also prototyped new systems. Friday morning strategic thinking blocks became nonnegotiable. No meetings before 9:00 a.m., to protect deep work time. Hard stop at 6:00 p.m., three days a week. Within two weeks, Max noticed his thinking getting sharper. The constant reactive pressure had been overloading the part of the brain responsible for strategic thinking and innovation. By creating predictable boundaries, he restored the cognitive bandwidth he'd been burning through with urgency and 24/7 availability.

Design → Build Integration Bridge: Max's clarity about his values and his vision for two horizons gave him the confidence to start prototyping immediately. Rather than waiting for perfect clarity, he tested new boundaries and volunteered for the AI exploration—turning insight into evidence that validated his direction. He cycled through multiple rounds of testing (boundary experiments, AI work exploration, strategic thinking routines), each iteration generating data that refined his approach.

REFINING DESIGN, RAMPING BUILD, EARLY LAUNCH

The prototypes generated learning. The AI work confirmed Max's direction—it was ambitious and strategic, required small-team collaboration, and sat at the innovation edge. This was the summit he wanted. His new routines worked. His team adapted without performance suffering. Data validated his design.

What struck him was the quality of the challenge. Max had always thrived under pressure, but this felt different—sharper, cleaner. In his current role, success came with organizational friction: politics, firefighting. The AI work was hard in a way that energized him. His thinking stayed crisp for hours. His body felt alert but not wired.

He recognized the sensation from earlier in his career—before the complexity of scale had layered on and he felt that organizational, red-tape drag. His nervous system was telling him something his ambition already knew: This wasn't just the next role. This was the right direction—the next big summit.

Max refined his vision based on this evidence. The AI product team became his target. He clarified scope: what was in (strategic innovation, small teams, emerging tech expertise) and what was out (politics-heavy work, sixty-plus-hour weeks, narrow career paths that would limit future options).

He mapped challenges. His reflexes under pressure were control and speed. When uncertain, he tried to force clarity by moving faster. This had served him well in the past, but advisory-style strategic leadership required patience and tolerance for ambiguity. Recognizing this pattern gave him awareness to interrupt it.

Build intensified. Max developed skills for the work ahead: asking better questions instead of providing all the answers, building influence without positional authority, and thinking systemically about product strategy in emerging tech. He practiced these skills in his AI exploration work.

He also started early Launch moves. Exploratory conversations with leadership about the AI team. Relationship-building with potential team members. Rollout planning for transitioning his current responsibilities.

Build → Launch Integration Bridge: The prototypes generated data Max couldn't ignore. His new routines worked, the AI work energized him, and his team adapted without performance suffering. Multiple Build cycles—prototyping boundaries, developing advisory-style leadership skills, building relationships with the AI team—gave him the conviction and evidence he needed to formally approach leadership about the transition.

ALL THREE PHASES RUNNING

With clarity established and prototypes validated, Max made his move. He approached leadership about officially transitioning to lead the AI product initiative. His pitch was clear: He'd earned the right to take this risk, and he wanted to do it in a way that modeled sustainable high performance.

Rollout became deliberate. Max transitioned current responsibilities over three months, finishing strong rather than checking out. He built his AI team carefully, prioritizing people over process. He set boundaries from day one. Strategic focus, not tactical firefighting. Collaborative decision-making, not command-and-control.

Connection mattered during the transition. Max's wife became his accountability partner for maintaining boundaries. His mentor check-ins increased. Close colleagues held space for both the uncertainty and the excitement.

Reflection happened continuously. Max kept a simple weekly journal and asked himself questions: What energized me? What drained me? What would I do differently? This wasn't just therapeutic—it was how learning stuck. Each week, he captured insights, and during sleep, his brain consolidated those experiences into long-term memory. The reflection practice accelerated his growth more than any leadership course could have.

Systems scaled with him. The routines he prototyped became team culture. His leadership modeled that sustainable excellence was possible. Strategic thinking time became protected across the team. Deep work mattered more than constant availability.

Throughout, Design work continued. Max kept refining his long-term vision based on what he was learning. Board inquiries started coming in. Advisory conversations emerged. He adjusted his ambitions—maybe it would take five years to reach the next chapter, not seven. The AI work was positioning him exactly as he'd hoped.

Launch → Design Integration Bridge: Twelve months in, Max didn't just change roles—he proved a new model of ambitious leadership. The systems he prototyped became team culture, the boundaries he tested became sustainable practice, and the vision he designed became the reality he's living. Now, he's back in Design, looping through the Design-Build-Launch growth cycle again—exploring board opportunities, prototyping advisory relationships, and building toward the next summit after this one.

THE TRANSFORMATION

Twelve months after he sought out coaching, Max reflected on what changed.

He didn't leave his company. He didn't blow everything up. He evolved within the structure by redesigning how he worked and what he worked on.

The AI initiative is thriving—small team, big ambition, exactly what he designed for. He's working on the hardest problems of his career, and he's energized rather than exhausted. He's thinking strategically at a level he couldn't access when buried in execution. He's building expertise in emerging tech that will be valuable wherever he goes next.

Board inquiries have turned into real conversations. His reputation as a strategic thought leader is expanding. The flexibility he designed for is materializing faster than expected.

The boundaries he created have allowed for more quality time with his family.

Max didn't just find his next summit. He designed a path that leads to multiple summits beyond. And he proved that ambitious leadership and sustainable work aren't contradictory—they're complementary when designed intentionally. It was *both and*, and not a choice of *either, or*.

THE NEXT CHAPTER

Max continues moving through Design-Build-Launch cycles. Now, he's designing what comes after the AI work. Exploring board opportunities. Prototyping advisory relationships. Building toward long-term freedom and impact that compounds.

The framework adapts with him. Each cycle builds on the last. Each iteration reveals new possibilities. This isn't a onetime transformation; it's a practice he'll use for every next big thing he creates.

Max didn't just climb the next mountain. He learned how to keep climbing—with intention, sustainability, and the freedom to choose his own summits.

Client Scenario 2

ALEX: FROM CAREER SUNSET TO CREATING HIS DREAM LIFE

Alex is in his early sixties, on the edge of retirement after more than thirty years leading marketing teams at a global hotel chain. He fell into corporate hospitality after school, loved the benefits—the travel, the compensation, and the stability—and now, he's ready to create his next big chapter.

For decades, Alex has been a consummate traveler, photographer, and foodie. Every vacation became a photo essay. Every destination became a story about place, culture, and cuisine. He quietly built a portfolio—published a few pieces, grew a modest following online, and documented stunning moments across dozens of countries. The creative work has always been there, thriving alongside his corporate career.

Now, with retirement on the horizon, Alex has more options than he knows what to do with. He's not in a rush, and that's become part of the problem. He's been spinning on a roundabout for a few years, exploring possibilities without committing to direction.

Alex lives with his life partner, no kids, and more freedom than he's ever had before to design what comes next. His values are clear. Freedom to move and create without corporate constraints. Beauty in the work he produces and the life he lives. Craftsmanship in his photography and storytelling. Connection and community as he gets older. He doesn't want to create alone or age in isolation.

The possibilities are endless. Move to Spain, where he's fallen in love with the progressive culture, arts scene, and food traditions? Stay in the US but shift his creative work from hobby to primary focus? Sell his home or rent it out for flexibility? Launch a travel memoir? Build a consulting practice? Go full-time as a photographer and writer? Open a gallery? Start a blog with serious intention? Step back and ease into a slower pace?

He's been exploring all of his options. And he's stuck, choosing none of them.

That's what brought him to coaching—not crisis but clarity. He's wondered: How do I design this next chapter so it honors my creative side and my values? How do I choose from all of these possibilities without paralyzing myself or making a decision I'll regret? How do I stop spinning and start building?

THE CCM IN ACTION

Alex worked through the Design-Build-Launch framework over nearly twenty-four months—starting before retirement and continuing through his transition to Spain. The method is agile. We started with clarity work in Design to break the paralysis of too many options, then quickly moved into Build and Launch to test possibilities and generate momentum. Each phase informed the others. Action created clarity. Data eliminated options that looked good in theory but didn't work in practice.

THE START: HEAVY DESIGN, STRATEGIC BUILD

We began with foundational clarity. Alex completed the Cloudberry values assessment, confirming what mattered most to him in this next chapter.

Six values rose to the top:

- Freedom—autonomy over his time, location, and creative choices
- Beauty—surrounding himself with art, culture, and aesthetic richness
- Craftsmanship—producing work that met his own high standards
- Connection—genuine relationships with creative peers and community
- Curiosity—continuous learning and exploration through travel and art
- Legacy—creating work that would outlast him and contribute to the world

These values became his decision filter. Any option had to honor most of them, or it wasn't worth pursuing. The roundabout he'd been spinning on suddenly had clearer exits. Consulting for hospitality brands? High income potential but low freedom and beauty. Opening a gallery in Spain? High beauty and connection but questionable financial sustainability. Going full-time as photographer and writer with strong online presence? Hit all six values if structured well.

From values, vision emerged. Alex painted what the next decade could look like. Living in Spain with his partner, embedded in a progressive arts community. Creating photography and travel writing that combined his hospitality expertise with his creative eye. Building an online presence that generated income and connection without corporate constraints. Using his hotel benefits to travel regularly and document culture, food, and place. Contributing to something larger than himself—beauty, storytelling, and community.

Ambitions became specific. Move to Spain within eighteen months. Rent his home, at first, as a fallback plan. And if all looks good, sell his US home to fund a new home and eliminate ties. Build a sustainable online presence through newsletters, blogs, and social media. Join or create a collaborative studio space with other artists. Maintain financial stability through photography sales, writing income, and strategic consulting. Adopt dogs—connection, routine, and movement mattered as he aged.

Identity work was essential. Who was Alex becoming? For thirty years, he'd been a corporate marketing executive who traveled and created on the side. That identity was ending. He named the new one: creative professional building legacy through beauty and storytelling. This required releasing the security of the corporate identity and trusting that his creative work could sustain him financially and emotionally. It also meant releasing ties with former coworkers, a major part of his community throughout his life.

While clarity work continued, Alex started prototyping immediately. Waiting until retirement to test ideas felt risky—better to experiment while he still had income stability.

He prototyped building online presence. He started a newsletter sharing travel photography and stories about food and culture. He posted consistently on social media, not just randomly. He tracked what resonated—which images, which stories, and which themes. The data was immediate. His audience grew. People engaged. But more importantly, Alex noticed something: Consistent creation energized him. His brain was wired for novelty and beauty. Producing work regularly activated reward systems that corporate work never had. He wasn't just creating; he was feeding something essential.

He also prototyped the Spain option. He and his partner spent four months there, not as tourists but as residents. They rented, explored neighborhoods, visited galleries, connected with local artists, researched visa requirements, and calculated cost of living. Theory became reality. Spain wasn't just romantic—it was logistically viable. The arts scene was vibrant. The cost of living was manageable. The culture fit their values.

Alex felt it in his body, too. For thirty years, he had carried a low-grade tension he'd stopped noticing—the corporate armor, the performance of executive presence, the relentless efficiency, and the identity defined by productivity metrics and stock price fluctuations. During those months in Spain, something released. His creative work flowed without the underlying current of guilt. His morning walks through the orange groves of Valencia felt expansive. His time was his own instead of 24/7 on someone else's clock. His hands just seemed steadier with his camera. Ideas for future blog posts flowed effortlessly.

His sleep was deeper. His heart felt full, and his intuition was no longer questioning on an endless roundabout circling too many possibilities. When he and his partner talked about making the change permanent, his chest opened instead of tightened. And a big smile instantly spread across his face. His body wasn't just saying this was viable; it was saying this is what freedom feels like.

Design → Build Integration Bridge: Alex's values work cut through years of spinning. Freedom, beauty, craftsmanship, connection, curiosity, and legacy—these became his decision filter. The month in Spain and the newsletter launch weren't just single prototypes. They were the beginning of multiple testing cycles that generated evidence about whether this dream was viable or fantasy. Each iteration refined his understanding of what a sustainable creative life actually required.

REFINING DESIGN, RAMPING BUILD, EARLY LAUNCH

The prototypes generated critical learning. The online presence worked. Alex's newsletter subscribers grew to two thousand, his social media following expanded, and brands started reaching out about collaborations. Spain felt right. The four months there confirmed it wasn't just a vacation fantasy but genuinely aligned with Alex and his partner's values.

Alex refined his vision based on evidence. He didn't need to choose between all of the options; he could integrate the best parts. Move to Spain for the lifestyle and community. Build online presence for income and creative outlet. Use hotel benefits for continued travel and content creation. Collaborate with other artists for connection and inspiration.

He clarified scope: what was in (creative work with aesthetic and narrative integrity, collaborative community, location flexibility, and income that supported his lifestyle without corporate grind) and what was out (corporate consulting that drained creativity, geographic ties that limited freedom, and isolation in his creative work).

He mapped challenges. His reflex under uncertainty was analysis paralysis—researching endlessly without committing. When faced with big decisions, he spun rather than chose. Recognizing this pattern gave him awareness to interrupt it. When he felt the urge to research one more option, he could pause and ask: Is this generating useful data or avoiding commitment?

Build intensified. Alex deliberately developed skills: consistent content creation, social media strategy, newsletter growth tactics, photography sales processes, building relationships with galleries and chefs and restaurants, and managing freelance income. He practiced these skills while still employed, building capability before he needed to rely on it.

He also built systems. Alex created a content calendar—three monthly newsletter editions, three weekly social media posts, and quarterly photo projects. He set up financial tracking to separate his creative income from his corporate salary. He built routines that protected creative time even while he was working full-time. These systems weren't just organizational—they were retraining his brain. When consistent creation became habit rather than willpower, it freed cognitive resources for higher-level creative thinking.

Early Launch moves started. Alex gave notice at work—eighteen months out, which gave him time to transition well and build financial runway. He listed his home for sale. He and his partner started serious visa applications for Spain. He reached out to artists' collectives in Valencia about studio space.

Build → Launch Integration Bridge: The prototypes generated momentum through repeated cycles of testing and learning. Newsletter subscribers grew, multiple Spain visits confirmed cultural fit, and his photography started attracting paid opportunities. Each Build cycle—content creation experiments, financial modeling, relationship building with Valencia artists—eliminated paralysis and gave Alex the confidence to retire, sell his home, and move with clear systems already in place.

ALL THREE PHASES RUNNING, MAJOR LAUNCH

With clarity established and prototypes validated, Alex made the big moves. He retired. His home sold quickly, providing capital for the Spain transition. He and his partner moved to Valencia, found an apartment in a vibrant arts district, and joined a collaborative studio space with painters, sculptors, and photographers.

Rollout was deliberate but exciting. Alex didn't try to have everything perfect before moving—he built as he went. He established routines in Spain: morning coffee and creative work, walking to the gym, afternoon studio time with collaborators, evening walks exploring the city. His newsletter evolved—more focused on the intersection of food, culture, and visual storytelling. His social media presence grew as he documented the transition. He started attracting the attention of other expats who desired his knowledge.

Connection became central to this new life. The studio collective provided daily creative community—critique, collaboration, and inspiration. Alex and his partner built friendships with local artists and expats. They adopted two dogs from a local rescue—connection, routine, and joy rolled into daily walks through Valencia's streets.

Alex's hotel benefits became strategic rather than just personal. He traveled regularly—train rides to Barcelona, Madrid, and Paris; flights to London and Berlin—and documented boutique hotels, food culture, and urban design. Each trip generated content for his newsletter and social media. His hospitality expertise gave him access and perspective others didn't have. Brands started paying for his photography and travel writing.

Reflection happened weekly. Alex kept a simple practice, asking himself questions such as: What did I create this week? What energized me? What felt forced? What wants to evolve? This wasn't just journaling—it was how learning consolidated. Each week, he captured insights about which content resonated, which collaborations worked, and which routines supported his creativity. His brain processed these patterns, turning trial and error into genuine expertise.

Systems scaled with him. The content calendar became automatic. Financial tracking showed which income streams worked. His creative routines became nonnegotiable. Alex's brain had literally rewired itself—what once required enormous effort now felt natural. The identity shift from corporate executive to creative professional wasn't just a mindset shift—it was neurological.

Throughout, Design work continued. Alex kept refining what this chapter could become. Maybe a photo book eventually. Maybe teaching workshops. Maybe deeper collaboration with hospitality brands. The vision kept evolving as he lived it.

Launch → Design Integration Bridge: Eighteen months into Valencia life, Alex didn't just retire—he designed freedom. The routines he prototyped became sustainable rhythms, the studio collective he joined became genuine community, and the creative work he'd kept in the margins became the center of a life built entirely on his terms. Now, he's back in Design, looping through the Design-Build-Launch growth cycle again. He's exploring what deeper creative work could look like, designing workshops and exhibitions, and building the next expression of a life lived beautifully.

THE TRANSFORMATION

Nearly twenty-four months after seeking out coaching—six months into life in Spain—Alex reflected on what changed.

He didn't just retire. He designed a life that honored everything he valued. He's living in Valencia with his partner and their two dogs. His studio collective provides daily creative community. His newsletter reaches five thousand subscribers and generates meaningful income through paid subscriptions and brand partnerships. His photography has been featured in travel publications. His social media documents a life of beauty, curiosity, and craftsmanship.

More importantly, Alex stopped spinning. He moved from paralysis caused by too many options to the clarity of aligned action. He's not wondering "what if" anymore—he's living it.

THE NEXT CHAPTER

Alex continues moving through Design-Build-Launch cycles. Now, he's designing what deeper creative work could look like—a photo book exploring boutique hotel design across Europe, teaching visual storytelling workshops for hospitality professionals, or maybe curating exhibitions in his studio space and adding a location.

The framework adapts with him. Each cycle builds on the last. Each iteration reveals new possibilities. This isn't a onetime retirement transition; it's a practice he'll use for every evolution ahead.

Alex didn't just retire from corporate life. He learned how to design freedom and order—a framework with beauty, connection, craftsmanship, and the courage to choose himself and his family.

Client Scenario 3

JEN: FROM FOLLOWING EXPECTATIONS TO REDEFINING IDENTITY AND SUCCESS

Jen is in her early forties with a successful career, stable income, and a life that looks good on paper. But lately, she's been asking hard questions.

Twenty years ago, she made practical choices. Marriage. Family. A job that paid well and offered security. At the time, those choices made sense. Graduate school could wait. Her intellectual pursuits could be put on hold. There would be time later.

Except later never came.

Now, two decades later, Jen's realizing something. Her life is good—really good. Stable marriage. Healthy kids. Solid career. But she's started wondering: What about what I want? She's been so focused on building this life that she hasn't stopped to ask what comes next for her. Not for her family. Not for her job. For her.

She's productive but disconnected at work. Present but distracted at home. Her marriage has become logistics rather than partnership. Her health has slipped. Her energy is low.

She wants time and space to figure out her next moves—in her career, in her personal life, in what fulfillment actually looks like when she's the one defining it.

That's what brought her to coaching—seeking clarity through questioning: Whose version of success have I been living? What would it look like to define success for myself? Who am I beyond the roles I've been performing? What's next for me?

THE CCM IN ACTION

Jen worked through multiple Design-Build-Launch cycles over eight months. The method is agile and configurable. We focused on the elements that actually resonated with her, not forcing frameworks that felt inauthentic. For Jen, vision and mission work felt cringy and prescriptive—more "shoulds" piled onto decades of living by others' expectations. Instead, we focused on values, purpose, and possibilities. Each cycle was quick (sometimes weekly, sometimes monthly), continuously refining her direction based on what she learned.

VALUES AND PURPOSE CLARITY

We began with values. Jen completed the Cloudberry values assessment, identifying what mattered most to her now versus what had mattered when she made those practical choices twenty years ago.

Six values emerged:

- Intellectual engagement—she needed work that challenged her mind instead of just filling her calendar.
- Authenticity—she wanted to show up as herself, not perform roles.
- Growth—she craved learning and evolution, not stagnation.
- Partnership—she wanted her marriage to be mutual, not one-sided logistics.
- Self-care—she needed to prioritize her health and well-being instead of just managing everyone else's.
- Agency—she wanted to make choices for herself rather than default to what seemed expected.

Seeing these values written down triggered something physical. Jen actually felt relief for the first time in months. She took a few deep breaths. It was recognition. Her body had been whispering these truths for years—through quiet pulls toward certain work, through the warmth in her heart when she imagined going back to school, through the way her energy lifted when conversations turned toward growth and learning. Her heart knew these values before her mind could name them. Seeing them written down felt like finally listening to what her intuition had been saying all along. It was guiding her. Her nervous system had been carrying the weight of misalignment for years. Naming what mattered gave her brain permission to stop fighting itself.

Purpose work came next. Why did reclaiming herself matter? Jen's answer was immediate: "So my daughter sees that women can build full lives that include their own dreams—not someday but now." This wasn't abstract future-gazing. This was about the example she was setting today.

While this clarity work continued, Jen started prototyping immediately. She signed up for an online course—just one evening a week—in a subject that had always fascinated her. She carved out thirty minutes each morning before everyone else woke up to drink coffee and think. She started saying no to committees that drained her.

These weren't grand gestures—they were experiments. Each time she held a boundary, her brain fired new neural pathways. Repetition was making the new behavior less foreign and more automatic.

EXPANDING POSSIBILITIES

The first prototypes generated learning. The online course lit her up. The morning routine became sacred. Her boundaries worked. Her family adapted, and her guilt decreased.

This evidence opened possibilities work. What could be different? Jen explored. Go back to school part-time. Shift her career toward something intellectually engaging. Reclaim hobbies she'd abandoned.

The goal wasn't picking one path; it was remembering what used to light her up and imagining what could light her up now.

She also worked on scope—what was realistic given her current life. What was in: intellectual engagement, authentic relationships, health prioritization, and agency. What was out: performing roles, endless accommodation, and self-abandonment disguised as selflessness.

She started bigger prototypes. She explored whether grad school was financially viable. She had honest conversations with her husband about what needed to change in their marriage—not blaming him but inviting partnership. She started exercising again because movement made her feel alive.

Design → Build Integration Bridge: Naming her values and acknowledging twenty years of misalignment gave Jen permission to act. The online course, the morning routine, and the small boundaries were prototypes that each tested whether reclaiming space was possible or just wishful thinking. She cycled through multiple rounds of foundation.

BUILDING SYSTEMS

With possibilities clarified and bigger prototypes validating her direction, Jen moved into sustained Build work. She enrolled in graduate school part-time. She renegotiated responsibilities at home—her husband took on more as his share, not a favor. She set clearer boundaries at work.

Systems became critical. The morning routine became nonnegotiable. Exercise happened before negotiation. Weekly reflection consolidated learning—what made her feel alive, what drained her, what wanted to evolve. Her brain was learning to recognize patterns and trust her desires.

Connection deepened. Her two close friends became her support system. She and her husband started weekly conversations about their marriage, not logistics. Her coach remained the consistent impartial presence.

PROFESSIONAL PIVOT

With grad school energizing her and her values clarified, Jen started noticing misalignment at work differently. It wasn't just mental—her body told her. Projects that engaged her intellectually left her energized. Bureaucratic tasks that once seemed fine now felt draining.

She began strategic networking—not random coffee chats but intentional connections with people in roles that aligned with her values. She leaned into allies who'd championed her work. She had honest conversations about what she actually wanted: intellectual engagement, growth opportunities, flexibility for graduate work.

Within six months, an opportunity surfaced: a role at a different organization that valued advanced education, rewarded intellectual contribution, and offered tuition support for her master's program with a path toward her PhD. The position wasn't a massive leap in title, but it was a profound leap in alignment.

Jen negotiated terms that honored her priorities: flexibility for coursework, work that challenged her mind, and a culture that saw her graduate education as an asset rather than a distraction. When she accepted the offer, her body knew before her mind could articulate it: This was what choosing herself felt like.

Build → Launch Integration Bridge: The prototypes proved it was possible. Her family adapted, her energy increased, and the intellectual engagement she'd been missing returned. Multiple cycles of building and testing—grad school exploration, boundary experiments, marriage conversations—gave her the evidence and courage to fully commit.

LAUNCHING AND INTEGRATING

With systems in place and evidence mounting, Jen launched fully into her redesigned life. Graduate school felt like coming home to herself. Her marriage shifted from logistics to genuine partnership—not without friction but with real effort from both sides. Her work performance improved because she was engaging rather than going through the motions.

Launch → Design Integration Bridge: Throughout all of this, Design work continued in small ways. Jen kept refining what she wanted based on what she was learning. The flexible structure felt like freedom.

THE TRANSFORMATION

Six months after she sought out coaching, Jen reflected on what changed.

She redesigned how she showed up. She set boundaries. She said no. She started pursuing things that engaged her intellectually. She went back to school part-time and felt alive in a way she hadn't in twenty years.

The other changes produced unexpected benefits. She felt more engaged at work—not because the job changed but because she was bringing more of herself to it. She felt more gratitude for what she had instead of focusing on what was missing. She felt more connected—to her work, to her purpose, to herself. Her manager noticed the shift. Opportunities started appearing that matched her newly identified interests.

Her marriage shifted. Her husband had to adjust to her taking up more space, and it wasn't always smooth. But they're rebuilding genuine partnership. Her daughter noticed—she said, "Mom, you seem happier."

Jen didn't just add graduate school to her life. She reclaimed her sense of self. And that changed everything.

THE NEXT CHAPTER

Jen continues moving through Design-Build-Launch cycles. Now, she's designing what professional work could look like if she fully leveraged her graduate education and newfound clarity. Exploring options that genuinely excite her. Prototyping conversations that feel aligned rather than obligatory. Building toward a version of success that's hers—not borrowed, not expected, but authentically chosen.

The framework adapts with her. Each cycle builds on the last. Each iteration reveals new possibilities and deepens her sense of agency. This isn't a onetime transformation; it's a practice she'll use for every next chapter she creates.

Jen didn't just figure out what's next. She learned how to keep designing what's next—with intention, agency, and fulfillment. She's happier now because she's living a life that reflects her values, engages her mind, and honors who she is. That's the shift that matters.

Client Scenario 4

MARIA: FROM ORGANIZATIONAL GROWING PAINS TO A LEADER WHO BUILDS CAPACITY IN OTHERS

Maria has devoted fifteen years to ending homelessness in her city. Starting as a case manager, she now leads a coalition of service providers. She knows the work intimately—the crisis calls, impossible funding cycles, and profound joy when someone gets housed.

Maria is deeply mission-driven, but she's hitting a wall. Needs keep growing while resources stay flat. She's carrying her organization's weight, making nearly every decision and fighting every fire, because who else will do it?

Her board asks hard questions about strategy and growth, but Maria feels stuck in survival mode. She's excellent at direct service but needs to evolve as a leader—delegating more, thinking systemically, building stronger teams, and creating sustainable impact rather than heroic intervention.

Maria can't afford executive coaching, yet she must grow as a leader to keep pace. Her organization operates on razor-thin margins. But investing in leadership development isn't selfish—it's strategic.

That's what brought her to pro bono coaching—not burnout (yet) but deeper questions: How do I scale my impact without scaling my hours? What would sustainable leadership look like? How do I build systems that work without me when I'm unavailable?

Through the CCM, Maria is building sustainable practices that energize both her mission-driven work and her own well-being.

THE CCM IN ACTION

Maria worked through the Design-Build-Launch framework over twelve months, moving through iterative cycles. The method is agile. We started with clarity work in Design but quickly moved into Build and Launch because Maria needed sustainable change, not just insight. Each phase informed the others. Small systems changes generated capacity. Data revealed what actually worked.

THE START: HEAVY DESIGN, EARLY BUILD

We began with foundational clarity. Maria completed the Cloudberry values assessment, identifying what mattered most to her in this season of leadership.

Six values emerged, revealing both her strengths and her challenges:

- Service—she was called to help people experiencing homelessness, full stop.
- Impact—her work needed to create measurable change, not just activity.
- Sustainability—she couldn't keep operating at this pace without breaking.
- Community—she valued collaboration and collective impact over solo heroics.
- Growth—she needed to develop as a leader, not just maintain what existed.
- Integrity—the work had to align with her values, even when funding pressures pushed compromise.

The tension was real. Maria valued both heroic service and sustainability. Both immediate impact and long-term growth. She'd been optimizing for service and impact while sacrificing sustainability and her own growth. That imbalance was burning her out and limiting her organization's potential.

From values, vision emerged. Maria didn't want to leave nonprofit work—she needed to lead it differently. Her vision was growing an organization that created lasting impact without requiring her constant intervention. Leading a team that was empowered and capable, not dependent on her for every decision. Creating systems that could scale beyond her personal capacity.

Ambitions became specific. Become more of a coach and mentor to build more capability and a leadership team that can operate independently. Create systems and processes that reduce daily firefighting. Develop strategic thinking capacity beyond survival mode. Protect time for her own health and relationships.

Identity work was critical. Who was Maria? She'd built her identity on being the person who never says no, who always shows up, who carries the weight. But that identity was tanking her energy and limiting her organization. She named a new one: strategic leader who builds capacity in others. This required acknowledging that her heroic intervention pattern wasn't just exhausting; it was preventing her team from developing and her organization from scaling.

While clarity work continued, Maria started prototyping immediately. Waiting wasn't an option. The work demanded action.

She prototyped delegation. She identified three decisions she made daily that her deputy director could handle. She handed them over with clear parameters and support. This felt terrifying—her instinct was to control everything. But her brain needed to learn that letting go didn't equal failure. Each time her deputy made a solid decision, Maria's nervous system updated its threat assessment.

She felt it in her body immediately. The hypervigilance that had become her baseline—always scanning for the next crisis, the next failure, the next thing only she could fix—dimmed. Her breath came easier. The chronic tension across her upper back, the kind that had her waking up sore every morning, started to release. For years, her body had been running a constant alarm: If you stop, if you delegate, everything collapses. But watching her deputy handle decisions competently, her nervous system was learning something new: Letting go wasn't abandonment. It was leadership. The relief wasn't just mental—it was physical. Her body was finally downshifting from emergency mode into something sustainable. She could feel the difference between carrying everything and building capacity in others. One exhausted her. The other freed her.

Delegation became less scary and more automatic.

She also prototyped boundaries. She stopped checking her email after 8:00 p.m. She blocked out Friday afternoons for strategic thinking instead of filling them with meetings. These choices felt impossible initially—nonprofit culture glorifies martyrdom. But boundaries weren't selfish. When Maria protected recovery time, her strategic thinking actually improved. Her prefrontal cortex needed breaks to function well. Running on constant urgency was impairing exactly the cognitive capacity she needed most.

Design → Build Integration Bridge: Clarifying her values exposed the core tension in Maria's leadership: She was trying to deliver impact while sacrificing sustainability. Naming that tension shifted her self-perception—from the person who must carry everything to the leader who builds capacity in others. Once Maria understood that sustainability was part of her mission, she entered Build with permission to act differently.

REFINING DESIGN, RAMPING BUILD, EARLY LAUNCH

The prototypes generated critical learning. Delegation worked. Her deputy director stepped up. The decisions were solid—sometimes better than Maria's would have been, because her deputy had different expertise. The boundaries held. The organization didn't collapse when she stopped being available 24/7. Data validated that sustainable leadership was possible.

Maria refined her vision based on evidence. She didn't need to do everything—she needed to build a team that could do things without her. She clarified scope: what was in (strategic leadership, systems building, team development, sustainable growth) and what was out (being the bottleneck, heroic intervention, saying yes to everything, sacrificing health for mission).

She mapped challenges. Her reflex under pressure was to take on more work herself rather than develop others' capacity. When crisis hit, she reverted to doing instead of delegating. When funding got tight, she cut her own salary before examining what programs actually created impact. Recognizing these patterns gave her awareness to interrupt them.

Build intensified. Maria deliberately developed skills: strategic delegation, systems thinking, developing others' leadership capacity, managing up with her board, protecting boundaries under pressure. She practiced these skills in real time, learning from what worked and what didn't.

She also worked on systems. Maria built a simple decision-making framework—level 1 involved decisions her team could make independently, level 2 needed check-ins, and level 3 required her involvement. This clarity freed her from constant decision-making and empowered her team. She created a weekly reflection practice—thirty minutes reviewing what worked, what didn't work, and which systems needed adjustment.

This reflection practice wasn't just cathartic—it was how learning stuck. Each week, Maria captured insights about which systems were working and what needed iteration. Her brain consolidated these patterns, turning trial and error into genuine organizational learning.

Early Launch moves started. Maria brought her leadership team into strategic planning instead of doing it alone. She presented a proposal to her board about building organizational capacity, not just serving more people. She started saying no to funding opportunities that didn't align with their strategic direction, even though saying no to money felt terrifying.

Build → Launch Integration Bridge: Maria's small experiments worked. Delegation held. Systems held. The organization didn't fall apart when she stepped back. Build gave her evidence—not hope—that sustainable leadership was possible. That evidence gave her the confidence to launch bigger changes: hiring a director of operations, restructuring her leadership team, and shifting from heroic intervention to distributed leadership.

ALL THREE PHASES RUNNING

With clarity established and prototypes validated, Maria made bigger structural changes. She hired a director of operations—not another service provider but someone to build systems. She restructured her leadership team with clear roles and decision-making authority. She implemented quarterly strategic planning sessions that weren't just reactive problem-solving.

Rollout was deliberate. Maria didn't overhaul everything at once—she built systems incrementally. First, decision-making clarity. Then, leadership team structure. Then, strategic planning rhythm. Each change built on the last, creating compounding impact.

Connection became essential during this transition. Maria built genuine relationships with peer nonprofit leaders who understood the unique pressures. She found a pro bono mentor—a retired nonprofit executive who'd built sustainable organizations and could offer perspective. Her coach remained her strategic partner, helping her see patterns and possibilities she couldn't see alone.

Reflection continued weekly. What systems were working? Where was she reverting to old patterns? What did her team need to grow? Each week Maria captured data, and over time, she started seeing what had been invisible before. Her heroic intervention pattern had triggers—certain types of crises, funding pressure, guilt about privilege. Naming these triggers reduced their power.

Systems scaled across the organization. The decision-making framework became team culture. Strategic planning sessions became quarterly rhythm. Boundaries around Maria's time became the organizational norm. The nonprofit sector's martyrdom culture was shifting, at least in her organization.

Throughout, Design work continued. Maria kept refining what sustainable nonprofit leadership could look like—not just for her organization but as a model for the sector. She started speaking at conferences about systems-building versus heroic intervention. The vision kept expanding.

Launch → Design Integration Bridge: Eighteen months later, she had built a sustainable model. The systems she prototyped became organizational infrastructure, the boundaries became cultural norms, and her team became the organization's greatest strength. From that stability, she reentered Design with a new question: How do we scale this impact beyond our city? The next cycle began—with a stronger foundation and wider ambition.

THE TRANSFORMATION

Eighteen months after seeking out coaching, Maria reflected on what changed.

She didn't leave nonprofit work. She didn't burn out. She rebuilt how her organization operated and how she led. Her leadership team is thriving—empowered, capable, making solid decisions independently. The organization is serving more people with better outcomes, but Maria is working fewer hours because systems are carrying the load. Her board recently approved salary for an intern—recognizing that her efforts were part of sustainability.

Beyond the organizational transformation, Maria's personal life shifted too. Her friends and family started including her more in plans because she could actually commit to showing up—and following through. She wasn't constantly in a state of panic, canceling at the last minute, or showing up physically but mentally still at work. She found more happiness as a byproduct of sustainable leadership. The joy she'd been chasing through heroic service had been waiting in the space she created by building systems and capacity in others.

More importantly, Maria proved that mission-driven work doesn't require martyrdom. She's building a model for sustainable nonprofit leadership that others are starting to follow.

THE NEXT CHAPTER

Maria continues moving through Design-Build-Launch cycles. Now, she's designing what regional impact could look like—how to scale the model beyond her city while maintaining quality and sustainability. Exploring partnerships with other nonprofits. Building systems that could be replicated across organizations. Growing impact without growing burnout—for herself or the sector.

The framework adapts with her. Each cycle builds on the last. Each iteration strengthens organizational capacity and her leadership. This isn't a onetime fix; it's a practice she'll use for every growth challenge ahead.

Maria didn't just save herself from burnout. She learned how to build sustainable impact—with systems, boundaries, and the courage to lead differently than the sector expects. And she's found more happiness along the way.

Client Scenario 5

JORDAN: FROM SOLO DRIVER TO COACHABLE LEADER

Jordan is a sharp, ambitious millennial leader known for pushing fast and getting results. After several high-impact roles, he's built a reputation for speaking up and challenging the status quo. Everyone wants Jordan on their projects and as a contributor.

He's ready for the next big chapter and yearns for promotion. He loves his boss, but in the job itself, the spark has faded. He has stayed longer than he should have out of loyalty, but it's creating quiet tension. The structure feels limiting.

Jordan is confident—sometimes to a fault. He's used to pushing through and delivering results. But now, he's getting constructive feedback around emotionally reactive moments, misreads with stakeholders, and bumping into blind spots. He's realized that effort alone isn't enough. He doesn't have many peers to unpack this with, and he needs an impartial partner—someone who's been where he wants to go next and can help him see what he can't see.

That's what brought him to coaching—questions about leadership development: How do I lead authentically without losing my edge and effectiveness? How do I grow into someone who's ready to be promoted and grow within the organization? What blind spots am I missing that everyone else can see? How do I reconnect with what energizes me, in work and in my personal life?

THE CCM IN ACTION

Jordan worked through multiple Design-Build-Launch cycles over twelve months. The method is agile and configurable. We focused on what actually worked for him, not forcing frameworks. For Jordan, vision work felt too abstract, like meditation. Not at all his thing.

Instead, we focused on values, purpose, and immediate skill-building. Each cycle was quick—sometimes weekly—and continuously refined new challenges based on what he learned.

THE START: VALUES AND PURPOSE

We began with values. Jordan completed the Cloudberry values assessment, identifying what actually mattered versus what he thought should matter.

Six values emerged:

- Impact—he needed to see tangible results.
- Recognition—he valued being seen for his contributions.
- Connection—despite his solo-driver reputation, he craved genuine relationships at work.
- Growth—he needed to be learning and developing, not stagnating.
- Trust—he wanted to be part of and build teams where the culture allows for taking risks that lead to bigger things.
- Fun—work needed to be engaging and energizing, not just grinding execution.

These values revealed something important: Jordan valued both driving hard and genuine connection. Both recognition and trust. He'd been optimizing for impact and recognition while neglecting connection, trust, and fun. That imbalance was showing up as friction—and limiting his promotion potential.

Purpose work came next. Why did getting to the next level matter? Jordan's answer was immediate: "I want to prove you can deliver exceptional results while building teams people actually want to work for—not just with." This wasn't abstract. This was about the kind of leader he wanted to become.

While clarity work continued, Jordan started prototyping immediately. Waiting wasn't his style. He prototyped slowing down in meetings—taking pauses and asking questions instead of jumping to solutions. He practiced vulnerability—admitting to a peer that he'd misread a stakeholder situation and asking for feedback.

His heart rate spiked when he said it out loud—that old pattern that equated honesty with weakness. But then, something shifted. His peer leaned in. The conversation deepened instead of collapsing. Jordan felt his breath settle, his posture open. His body was learning something his ambition had missed: Vulnerability wasn't liability. It was currency. The tightness he'd been carrying—that constant readiness to defend and challenge—wasn't protection. It was noise. His nervous system was updating in real time, and his body knew it before his mind could rationalize it.

He had an honest conversation with his boss about the role not fitting and his promotion ambitions.

Each time he chose the new pattern, his brain fired new neural pathways. Repetition was making coachability more automatic.

Design → Build Integration Bridge: Jordan's values work revealed the gap between impact and connection, recognition and trust. Understanding this gave him a clear target: Keep the drive and add the human skills. He cycled through multiple rounds of design to skill-building and testing—vulnerability experiments, meeting approaches, stakeholder conversations. Each iteration built capability and confidence.

BUILDING SKILLS

The first prototypes generated rapid learning. Slowing down improved outcomes. Vulnerability deepened relationships. His boss appreciated the honesty and started exploring internal opportunities.

Jordan refined his approach based on evidence. He worked on skills: active listening, emotional regulation under pressure, reading stakeholder dynamics, giving feedback without edge, and receiving feedback without defensiveness.

He also worked on challenges—his reflexes under pressure were to push harder and move faster. When stressed, he became controlling. Recognizing this pattern gave him awareness to interrupt it.

He built systems: ten minutes of daily reflection asking what went well, what went wrong, and what he'd do differently. This wasn't natural for Jordan—his instinct was to keep moving. But reflection was consolidating learning and turning experience into growth.

Build → Launch Integration Bridge: The prototypes worked faster than Jordan expected. People responded, relationships deepened, and his boss started seeing him differently. Multiple cycles of practicing new behaviors and getting feedback gave him the evidence and readiness to pursue the next big opportunity: an internal role that would reward both his execution strength and his evolving collaborative leadership.

INTERNAL TRANSITION

With skills developing and evidence mounting, an opportunity opened internally—a strategic initiative requiring cross-functional collaboration with real impact potential. Jordan pursued it actively.

Rollout was Jordan's strength. He transitioned cleanly from his current role. He built his new team by thoughtfully hiring for cultural fit and collaboration, not just skill. He set expectations from day one: move fast and deliver results while also building trust and connection.

Connection became central. Jordan built genuine relationships with peers. He scheduled regular check-ins to connect, not just to extract information. His coach remained his impartial partner, calling out blind spots without judgment.

SUSTAINING AND GROWING

With the new role launched, Jordan focused on sustaining the changes and continuing to grow. Daily reflection became automatic. His meeting approach—ask first, propose second—became default. Strategic pauses before reacting became reflex.

Throughout, small Design refinements continued. What kind of leader did he want to become? Not just effective—trusted. Not just fast—strategic. The vision evolved as he grew into it.

Launch → Design Integration Bridge: Twelve months in, Jordan's still getting results—but now in a way that builds trust and energizes teams. The coachability he developed became his competitive advantage, the self-awareness he built became his leadership edge, and the promotion he pursued became the launching pad for continued growth.

Now, he's back in Design, looping through the Design-Build-Launch growth cycle again—exploring what senior leadership could look like and designing how to scale his impact while maintaining the collaborative approach that unlocked this level.

THE TRANSFORMATION

Twelve months after seeking out coaching, Jordan reflected on what changed.

He didn't leave his company. He got promoted to a role that fit better and rebuilt how he showed up as a leader. His new team is thriving—engaged, collaborative, and delivering exceptional results without burning out. Stakeholder relationships are strong. His peers seek him out for partnership, not just execution. His boss recently told him he's become the kind of leader the organization wants to develop and promote further.

More importantly, Jordan's still getting stuff done—but now in a way that builds trust, energizes teams, and positions him for continued growth. People still want him on their projects, but now, they also want to work *for* him.

His relationships outside work improved too. He's more present. Less reactive. His girlfriend noticed he's easier to be around. His friendships deepened because he's connecting, not just networking.

Jordan leveraged his strengths while developing the capabilities that unlock his next level. And that changes everything going forward.

THE NEXT CHAPTER

Jordan continues moving through Design-Build-Launch cycles. Now, he's designing what senior leadership could look like—how to scale his impact while maintaining the collaborative, trust-based approach he's developed. Exploring options within his organization. Building relationships strategically. Growing intentionally toward roles that will challenge and energize him.

The framework adapts with him. Each cycle builds on the last. Each iteration reveals new capabilities and possibilities. This isn't a onetime fix; it's a practice he'll use for every leadership challenge and promotion ahead.

Jordan didn't just become a better leader. He learned how to keep becoming better—with self-awareness, collaboration, and the courage to see his blind spots before they limit him.

The Art of Integrated Coaching

As you've no doubt grasped from these scenarios, there's no single methodology that fully defines my approach to coaching. No one-size-fits-all formula could ever do justice to the complexity of the people I work with or the custom-tailored services that I provide them.

From my perspective, coaching is at its best and most effective when the focus is transformational, not transactional. I see the coaching services that I provide to my clients as an evolving, relational art form that's built on mutual trust, intuition, and timing. It's about letting the moment inform when to ask and when to listen, when to challenge and when to affirm, when to offer structure and when to simply hold space.

Because of this outlook, my coaching practice is built around a belief that people are inherently capable of more clarity, confidence, and impact when given the right support, tools, and conversation at the right time. That belief, forged through years in the crucible of leadership and tested across hundreds of coaching engagements, is the foundation of everything I do.

Whether I'm working with a high performer moving into their next big role, an executive facing reinvention, a client navigating burnout, or a human being simply trying to reclaim their vision and voice, my aim is to bring presence, perspective, and possibility into the room. To meet people exactly where they are and help them move powerfully toward where they want to be.

This palette of coaching styles, modalities, and frameworks doesn't represent a rigid process. Rather, it reflects a philosophy—one rooted in curiosity, shaped by experience, and guided by an unwavering respect for the human potential inside every client I serve.

At the end of the day, my coaching practice isn't really about me at all. Instead, it's about my clients—their growth, their agenda, their breakthroughs, and their progress.

And my commitment is to bring every tool, every lesson, every ounce of belief that I have to help each and every one of my clients write the next chapter of their lives as if it's their own—because it is.

CONCLUSION

YOUR NEXT BIG CHAPTER

So, there it is: the story of how I left the peak after decades in tech to set off on a journey of professional and personal growth, to confront the challenge of creating a brand-new version of myself, and to scale and summit the unexplored heights of the entrepreneurial coaching space. Along the way, I took my deep-rooted Midwestern values and combined them with all of the strategies I'd learned in my long career in tech and engineering to create the CCM.

Through my unique coaching method, I've been able to help a growing number of people face the crossroads in their lives, reassess their positions and expectations, and write the next chapters of their stories. It's been a life-affirming and satisfying journey for me to witness the remarkable progress that others have made by utilizing the CCM.

By working with my clients in a simple, repeatable arc (Design → Build → Launch. Repeat.), I've been able to create a framework that not only leads to professional growth and personal progress but also is essentially self-perpetuating, as each element feeds into the next and every step forward creates momentum that builds to greater and greater progress and achievement.

I've been able to further accelerate this forward movement for my clients by sharing with them an understanding of neuroscience and by applying advanced coaching tools. I've shown them the impact these tools have on each of us—not in the theoretical sense but in the very practical aspects of how each of us lives our day-to-day.

As a tech veteran and engineering leader by nature, it's always been essential for me to understand the why and the how of any system—and, certainly, to understand the mechanics that drive it.

I am excited for the next chapter (pun very much intended) of my life and the continuation of working with my clients through the life-changing steps of the CCM. There's nothing quite as fulfilling as seeing something I initially designed for my clients' growth be put into this book to help others.

And that's exactly the lesson that I want to leave you with.

I'm obviously an advocate of professional growth and self-improvement, however you might want to approach it. I think that becoming the best you that you can possibly be is a noble quest.

But here's the part that I think is the most effective: Perhaps the highest-return habit you can build isn't found in focusing on yourself but in serving someone else.

Even while I was intent on building my coaching business, I saw the chief reward as coming not in the form of my professional growth but in the significant impact I was having (and continue to have) on the lives of others.

That's why ever since the earliest beginnings of the CCM, I've been determined to bring my system to as many people as I possibly can. Today, almost one quarter of my professional time is pro bono, spent on and devoted to bringing the CCM to individuals who otherwise wouldn't be able to engage my services or training public service and charitable organizations to offer the benefits of the CCM to those whom they serve.

I don't offer this as a brag but as perhaps the most potent piece of advice that I hold in my considerable arsenal.

While the challenges of the modern age are undoubtedly significant and the rush to reach the summit of whatever mountain we happen to be climbing often seem pressing and all-encompassing, sometimes, the best thing you can do for yourself is to simply do something for someone else.

Service isn't charity on the margins; it's a performance enhancer for your life. When you help another person, you interrupt rumination, shrink fear, and expand agency. You create accountability outside yourself, you find perspective that your problems alone can't give, and you tap motivation that lasts longer than willpower. Paradoxically, one of the fastest ways to improve your own life is to invest in someone else's.

There's plenty of neuroscience to back this up, but we'll save that for a future volume.

For now, practice the part that matters: Improving the lives of others inherently improves your own.

And it's something that you can begin today, right now.

I certainly encourage you to reach out to me or to employ the tactics that I've set out here for yourself. But your road to writing your life and your next professional chapters—that journey to the top of the next mountain—is infinitely enhanced when you help others along the way.

Be kind. Take care of one another.

No matter how challenging the next summit appears, desolate your surroundings or how fierce the storms that batter you, be bold, be bright, be resilient—and always give back ... like the cloudberry.

ABOUT THE AUTHOR

Brad Lekang is the founder of Cloudberry Coaching and the author of *The Cloudberry Coaching Method: Design, Build, and Launch Your Next Big Chapter*, a groundbreaking guide for highly motivated individuals and driven leaders who are ready to design their next bold chapter. Drawing on over two decades of experience across Fortune 100 companies—most recently as a tech executive in Silicon Valley—and his deep roots in coaching, mentoring, and leadership development, Brad helps individuals craft meaningful and powerful transitions in both life and work. His leadership insights were forged both at Target and Visa and during his decades in tech, most recently leading technical teams at Apple—part of his dozen-plus years in Silicon Valley—where he helped launch consumer mobile products used by hundreds of millions across dozens of countries.

Brad blends technical design and development, coaching, mentoring, neuroscience, business strategy, and a human-centered approach to unlock transformation at every level. He believes we are all leaders—of something—in our professional or personal lives and brings that belief into every coaching conversation. His approach combines systems-thinking structure and rigor with coaching acumen, leadership development, and personal growth—an approach rooted in heart, challenge, optimism, and grit, with an abundance of whiteboard-fueled sessions that turn vision into action.

Brad is a Professional Certified Coach (PCC) with the International Coaching Federation and a Certified Professional Co-Active Coach (CPCC) through the highly acclaimed Co-Active Training Institute. He is also a Certified NeuroTransformational Coach (CTNC) through BEabove Leadership, widely recognized as the cutting-edge gold standard in advanced neuroscience-based coach training. Additionally, he holds an MBA from the University of Minnesota Carlson School of Management and a Stanford Advanced Project Management (SAPM) certification through Stanford University School of Engineering.

A proud Minnesotan with Norwegian roots, Brad lives in Minneapolis with his husband, Ken, and their yellow labs, Hazel and Otis. He still believes most problems can be solved—one conversation, multiple whiteboard brainstorming sessions, or a few national park visits at a time. He's visited forty-five of the sixty-three national parks and counting.

www.ingramcontent.com/pod-product-compliance
Lightning Source LLC
LaVergne TN
LVHW090601110826
845146LV00001B/216

* 9 7 9 8 8 9 1 8 8 1 8 5 3 *